Prayers For A Sojourning People

A Collection of Pastoral Prayers

by Susan Gregg-Schroeder

PRAYERS FOR A SOJOURNING PEOPLE
by Susan Gregg-Schroeder
© 1997 Susan Gregg-Schroder
Cover design by John C. Imel

ISBN 1-57438-015-X

Published by Educational Ministries, Inc.
800-221-0910
Contact the author at:
First United Methodist Church
2111 Camino del Rio South
San Diego, CA 92108
619-297-4366

Table of Contents

DEDICATION:

These prayers are dedicated to the congregation of San Diego First United Methodist Church for allowing me to walk with them as sojourners in faith.

Introduction

Prayer does not have to be eloquent to be prayer. It doesn't even have to be spoken. Paul said, the Spirit "intercedes for us" (Romans 8). You can pray sitting quietly, opening your life to God's presence.

Some people are given the gift of extempore prayer. I have been in meetings when the gathering became a community because of the prayer offered by a member. The words were addressed to God, not to us, but as they ascended they lifted us and made us one.

As vital to the life of the community is the formal prayer. It is like a concerto, or a sonnet, guided by rules that determine the structure. It contains prescribed elements: thanksgiving, confession, petition, dedication. Whoever attempts the formal prayer will follow the expected formula. If there is innovation, it is variation on the set theme.

There is a special type of formal prayer. It is called the "pastoral prayer." It is in the pattern of formal prayer, but you sense something more. It begins with personal spiritual discipline, the way an artist's work rests solidly on the practice of fundamentals. It requires participation in the suffering all human beings endure, the "groaning in travail" of the creation. It is nourished by daily contact with the congregation, sustained from understanding the seasons, absorbing the scriptures, and caring for the world.

Susan Gregg-Schroeder is a pastor. She has been given a spiritual gift, which she has disciplined into a craft, and God has matured that craft into its highest form, the pastoral prayer. All you need to do is read the prayers in this volume and you will sense their power.

They can be used as models for pastors ordering worship, or for one's personal devotion. In either case you will hear your needs as a person spoken and the assurance of the Gospel proclaimed.

Mark Trotter
Senior Minister
First UMC, San Diego, CA

Be a Sojourner

Liturgist: Come along with me
          as a sojourner in faith.
     Bring along
          a sense of expectancy
          a vision of high hopes
          a glimpse of future possibility
          a vivid imagination
   For God's creation is not done.

People: We are called to pioneer
          a future yet unnamed.
     As we venture forward,
          we leave behind our desires for
               a no-risk life
               worldly accumulations
               certainty.

Liturgist: Let us travel light
          in the spirit of faith and expectation
          toward the God of our hopes and dreams.

People: May we be witnesses
          to God's future breaking in.

Liturgist: Come along with me
          as sojourners in faith
          secure in the knowledge
          that we never travel alone.

God, we are sometimes overwhelmed by the awe, the wonder and the mystery of your presence in our lives. We do not know when you will appear to us, for you continue to surprise us by touching our lives in those unexpected sacred moments of wonder. You come to us at an hour we do not expect.

As we enter this season of Advent preparation, Divine Spirit, it is easy to get so caught up in the bustle of our day that we miss your presence in our midst. Slow us down. Still our anxious worries of what's left undone. Quiet our hearts to hear the inner rhythms of peace. Awaken in us a hope. Open us to the miracle of new possibilities for our lives.

Help us, O God, to not be so caught up in our own "busyness" that we are blinded to the needs of those for whom this season of joy and expectation might be especially difficult. Enable us to be candles in the dark to persons who are lonely, to those who are struggling with disease and illness, to those who grieve a loss, to those who have no place to call home, to those who are worried and anxious about the future, to those who are alienated from the ones they love, to those who are victims of oppression, injustice and violence. You alone are the source of our hope and our healing. Your presence continually reminds us of our connectedness to one another, and to you.

And so we wait...in patience...in expectation...in alertness...in anticipation. We sense that you are very near, and we await those holy moments when your love and light fill us with radiance and hope. Make ready our hearts to accept the gift of new life that is struggling to be born all around us. Amen.

Matthew 24: 36-44

O God, you make your presence known in so many ways...in a child lying in a manger...in a man dying on a cross. In this special season, we feel your presence in churches decorated for Christmas, in children gathering to sing carols, in the holiday preparations that are part of our homes. Help us, O God, to see you in other places as well...in the faces of the poor and homeless as they wait for help...in the efforts of our elected leaders to bring justice to a hurting world...in the hope of all persons who seek alternatives to war and violence...in the frenzy of shoppers to find gifts for friends and loved ones...in the labor of all persons who care for others...in the expectant eyes of children...in the tenderness of parents...in the patience of doctors and nurses...in the grace with which persons face illness and death.

Forgive us, Loving God, for our self-centeredness, our overwork and our weariness. Slow us down and help us to wait expectantly for your presence in all the unexpected and surprising places in our lives. Let this season be a time of deep spiritual renewal for each of us. Transform our vision to see the world as you see it. Bring hope and love and joy into our midst, that we might share with all the world a faith that encounters miracles of love and a belief that banishes sorrow. Amen.

oving God, we come before you in this season of Advent, this season of expectations, this season of joy, this season of hope, this season of new beginnings and birthing. It is hard for us to be in a mood of quiet anticipation when the shopping malls are already playing music proclaiming that Christ is born. It is hard to prepare our hearts to receive the gift of Emmanuel when the media and businesses are pulling out all the stops to boost sales and profits during this season. It is hard to hear the voice crying in the wilderness - a voice that calls us to repentance and to prepare the way of the Lord. It is hard to really examine our lives and discover those places where we need to turn around, to repent, to take a new direction.

Yes, it is hard. But we are here today gathered together in this place to open ourselves to yearnings we feel in our hearts, that this year, Emmanuel will come to us in a new and unexpected way. We come in the spirit of hope that what has been foretold and promised by the prophets can actually happen in our own lives. Some of us need to hear John's challenge and make significant changes in our lives. Others of us are hurting and need to be gathered in as a shepherd gathers sheep. We need to be held in your arms. We need to feel safe and secure in your presence. We need to know that whatever our situation, difficulty or sadness, we can trust in your knowing us by name, comforting us and accepting us just as we are.

And so we wait and watch. Enable us to be caught up in the mystery, awe and wonder of this season of preparation, for we seek a place to call home where your light directs our journey and where our hearts find shelter. Allow us to be vulnerable enough to see afresh the love born into the world in each moment, for you are a God of blessing and hope. Amen.

Isaiah 40:1-11

Mark 1: 1-8

God, this is a season of waiting...a season of expectation...a season of preparation for the coming of Emmanuel into our lives and into our world. We confess, O God, that we aren't very good at waiting. We wait in traffic, we wait in stores, we wait for doctor's reports and on and on. Sometimes we wait alone. At other times family and friends wait with us. Some waits have brought joy, some sadness. Some waits have been worth waiting for...others have not. And now it is Advent, and we find ourselves waiting again...waiting for your word to break into our lives in some unexpected way.

And so we pray that there might be meaning to this season of waiting. Enable us to use this time to make the necessary preparations to prepare a place in our hearts for the anticipated new birth. Help us to be honest with ourselves as we examine our lives. Give us the strength to make changes in our lives where necessary. And keep us awake and aware, O God, for this is the season when you take us by surprise and give us hope that everything can be made new again. In the spirit of hope, wonderment and anticipation, we lift our prayers to you.

We lift our prayers for those who walk in darkness, even in the shadow of death, that they might receive strength and comfort.

We lift our prayers for the poor, the persecuted, the sick, the homeless and all who suffer, that they might be relieved and protected.

We lift our prayers for those who have lost their way, that their lives might be illumined by the light of hope.

We lift our prayers for the church in this place and everywhere that it might be a source of hope and truth and light to the world.

And we lift prayers for ourselves that we might use this season of waiting to seek your presence in a deeper, more meaningful way.

As your children, O God, we wait. May our communion with you and with one another extend beyond the hymns and prayers and words spoken here. Be real in our midst. Christmas is coming and we seek a miracle. For yours is the kingdom of eternal light and joy. Amen.

oly God, in this season of waiting and anticipation, we lift to you the dreams and yearnings of our hearts. This is a season of hope and new beginnings. Fill us, we pray, with a passion for justice, a renewed commitment to mercy, and the love to work for reconciliation among those whose lives we are able to touch.

In the midst of frenzied holiday preparations, slow us down. Prepare in our hearts a warm and welcoming place that we might receive the gift of your son. Create in us a quiet place where these holidays can truly be holy days. As we think of giving gifts to others, we ask you, O God, for gifts that only you can give.

To those who are sick and facing an uncertain future, give the gift of a vision of healing and wholeness that is your desire for all creation. In your mercy, Lord, hear our prayers.

To those who are mourning and who face the holidays with mixed emotions, give the gift of a deepened awareness of your presence with them, as well as with the loved ones they miss so much. In your mercy, Lord, hear our prayers.

To those who are lonely, sorrowing or anxious, give the gift of your power, peace and patient endurance for these difficult times. In your mercy, Lord, hear our prayers.

To those who are out of work, those without a home to go home to this Christmas, and all who struggle with the reality of living day to day, give the gift of hope that doors will be opened in their future. In your mercy, Lord, hear our prayers.

To each one of us, O God, we pray that we might see afresh the love and wonder that is born into the world at each and every moment. In your mercy, Lord, hear our prayers.

May each of us welcome your Son, the Son before whom even the desert blooms and rejoices, with an open heart and a receptive spirit. For you send your gifts, not with ribbons and fancy wrapping, but with simplicity and humility. We give thanks for all your gifts of life. Amen.

Isaiah 35:1-10

Loving God, in this season of waiting and watching, we look to your coming to us once again. You come in the sound of silence and in the laughter of friends. You come in the darkened night by bringing joy to an unexpecting world. Sometimes we feel burdened down with our own sorrows and preoccupations and we miss your coming. And so we lift our prayers that you might break into our confusion and illumine our way.

We lift our prayers this day for those who struggle with illness, for those who grieve, for those who face difficult decisions, and we ask that you might touch the lives of those we name in our heart with renewed faith and hope.

We pray for the poor and the oppressed, for the unemployed and the homeless and for all who remember and care for them.

We pray for peace in the world and for the unity of all your people.

We pray for ourselves, for the forgiveness of our shortcomings and for the grace of the Holy Spirit to make changes in our lives where needed.

This Advent season is a time when your light radiates into our darkness. Help us to realize that in your light we are all connected to one another. Help us to use that light to guide others and keep them from danger. Keep us from growing weary of waiting for your love and light, lest we miss your coming into our lives and into our world. We know neither the day or hour of your coming, and we seek the hope and good news that wait to be born again in our hearts. Amen.

Mark 13:32-37

My soul magnifies you and my spirit rejoices in you, my God and my Savior, for you have regarded the low estate of us all and have called us blessed. You have done great things for us and holy is your name.

We approach this Christmas with a sense of awe and wonder, O God, for all that you have done for us. From you comes forth the one who shall govern your people. We give thanks that we may be numbered among those whom, through Christ, you have chosen. We seek to be faithful in all the areas of our lives. Help us to minister to others as Christ ministers to us.

Where persons are lost or bewildered, help us to stand as shining rays of hope. In your mercy, Lord, hear our prayers.

To those who wander aimlessly or who are unsure of themselves, help us to bring fresh esteem, clarity of mind and renewed purpose. In your mercy, Lord, hear our prayers.

For those who are suffering from spiritual pain or physical illness, help us to witness to your love and presence in their lives. In your mercy, Lord, hear our prayers.

For ourselves, O God, make us worthy in all that we do to receive the gift of your Son. In your mercy, Lord, hear our prayers.

And so we prepare ourselves to welcome the child born in Bethlehem. Our trembling anticipation is mixed with rejoicing and joy. Touch us just where we are, the way you touched Mary. Awaken in us new life. Stir in us fresh hope. Fill the dark spaces of our lives with your light...and your love. May we extend to all Christ's gift of new life. May our days be filled with moments of grace. May our nights be filled with the peace of the reconciled. We pray all this in the name of the one who comes to us in the stillness of the night and changes our lives forever. Amen.

Micah 5:2-5a

Luke 1:39-55

oving God, we anxiously await the birth of the Holy Child in our hearts. The moment draws closer and our hearts beat faster with anticipation. The waiting and preparation will soon be over. Our expectations are high, but, like Joseph, we are also timid and afraid. We don't know for sure how our lives will be changed with the coming of Emmanuel. We only know that if we truly seek to embrace the newborn babe, our lives will be forever changed. This Holy Child is the source of all joy and is our eternal hope. This Holy Child will bring light to the hidden corners of our lives. This Holy Child will touch us where we are wounded to bring healing and new life. This Holy Child will cause our hearts to leap in wonder and our souls to swell with love.

Fill us this day, O Holy One, with compassion for one another. We lift prayers for children bright with wonder as well as for those children without food to eat or a place to lay their heads; for those who have lost a loved one and who face this holy season with only their memories; for service men and women and their families who are separated this Christmas; for the sick, lonely and broken in our midst and for all peoples of the world struggling for life, livelihood, and a sense of purpose and justice. Help us to share the peace, hope and love of this season. May the coming of the Holy Child inspire us to new ways of relating to one another as broken relationships are made whole again.

And so we wait still. We seek signs and reassurances that the gift of Emmanuel will come to us. We seek to be restored by your grace and in your love so that we might truly appreciate and accept the precious gift we are about to receive. God of the Unexpected, surprise us once again with those moments of insight as we join our hearts and minds in joyful worship this day. Enable us to celebrate what has been even as we venture forward to celebrate what will be as witnesses and participants in the birth of a new humanity. O Come, O Come, Emmanuel. Amen.

Isaiah 7:10-17

Matthew 1:18-25

18

Divine Spirit, we humbly come before you in this most holy time of the year. Like Mary, our souls magnify you and our spirits rejoice in your presence, for you have looked with favor upon each of us. You have blessed us and done great things for us.

We also come before you, O God, with that unborn part of us leaping with joy and expectancy at the wonder of this birth, this new beginning, this coming of the Promised One. Just as you chose to bless Mary with birthing your son, so also you choose to bless each of us, no matter what our circumstances, no matter what our triumphs or failures, no matter whether we are rich or poor, young or old, no matter the color of our skin or the language we speak, no matter what past burdens or regrets we carry deep inside. Each of us is invited to kneel at the manger and to receive your gifts of love, grace and peace. Enable us to share in the simplicity of the stable, the innocence of a young girl, and the wonder of this birth. For it is in the still darkness of the night that we feel your hand holding ours, even as we feel the pangs of new birth and the struggle to breathe in the breath of life.

Let this season be a time of deep spiritual renewal for us all. Enable all who are sick, weary, lonely, or heavy laden, to look up and see the star shining brightly over the manger. Help us to see what gifts of ourselves we can offer to a hurting world in the name of the child who is for us the light of the world. Let the star that led the wise men to the stable, shine in our hearts and our imaginations this Christmas. Amen.

Micah 5:2-5a

Luke 2:1-7

Creator God, you are God of all beginnings...of fresh starts...of new chances...of all things made new. As we look ahead to this New Year, we also give thanks for the year past with all its joys and its sorrows. We are not the same persons that we were a year ago, and we are aware once more, O God, of the fleetingness of time - an awareness that calls us to make the most of every moment that you have given us.

As we look ahead, we ask that you help us to accept the difficult parts of our lives. Help us to overcome the fears that would keep us from living life abundantly. Help us to make the changes we need to make. Help us to let go of past regrets and failures so that we might move forward in new hope...that we might become the persons you would have us be.

The future is uncertain. We don't know what events lie ahead for us. But amidst all the tension of our world and the turmoil of our lives, you remain at the center, calling us to hope and to a renewed sense of purpose. In this new year, we pray for guidance for the nations of our world. Help us to truly be instruments of your peace as we seek to reach out to those in need, especially the young, the old, the tired, the poor, the sick and the grieving. Whatever comes our way in this new year, O God, we know that you are with us in all the times of our lives. For this we give you thanks.

May we be led to new places of openness and love toward you and the people around us. Enable us to do justice, to love mercy and to walk humbly before you in all that we do. Amen.

Micah 6:6-8

oving God, we have been touched by the joy of Christmas. You have filled us once again with the joy of living and the spirit of giving. Your promises have been fulfilled through the coming of the child, Emmanuel. Jesus was born of the flesh that we might be born of the spirit. May we be faithful to our birthright as we praise you for all you have done for us. You have shown us mercy through an abundance of steadfast love. You have saved us from trial and distress and brought us new hope and new life.

How comfortable and complacent we become as we bask in your gift of this child. We want to sit beside the manger and linger awhile. But the message of Christmas, O God of Love, is a message of moving on. The donkey awaits to carry us on a journey...a journey into uncertainty. Just as you meet us in the familiar places, so, too, do you call us out to far away places for our safety and for our growth. Help us to trust in your abiding love and to not turn away from any of the possibilities you have in store for us. For you will see us through our times of suffering and affliction. In response to your faithfulness, kindness and mercy, we lift our prayers this morning.

We lift prayers for all persons who are refugees, who are pulled away from the safety and security of home. In your mercy, Lord, hear our prayers.

We lift prayers for the hungry, for the poor in substance and spirit and for those who are without hope. In your mercy, Lord, hear our prayers.

We lift prayers for those who suffer from illness, for those who must face the future with the loss of a loved one and for those who seek your presence in a time of trial. In your mercy, Lord, hear our prayers.

We lift prayers for ourselves that we might meet the hard decisions and difficult challenges seeking first your guidance and will for our lives. In your mercy, Lord, hear our prayers.

May we be led to new places of openness, receptivity and love toward all the persons who touch our lives. And may we receive the gift of your vision that sees beyond what the world is and reaches out, restlessly, to what we can become. Amen.

Isaiah 63:7-9   *Matthew 2:13-15, 19-23*

A new day has dawned brightly, one filled with the promise of your presence with us. Darkness cannot overcome the light that you have brought into the word. And so, Loving Creator, even though the future is uncertain, we trust in your abundant grace and goodness. For when we have stumbled, you have provided a straight path. When we have wept, you have brought consolation. When we have lost our way, you have led us back. When we have been scattered in our daily living, you have gathered us back together again. When we have mourned, you have brought joy. When we have sorrowed, you have brought gladness. When we have thirsted for you, you have filled our empty souls with refreshment and nourishment. When we have been in darkness, your light has shined in our darkness and we were not overcome. When we were living in despair and doubt, your word became flesh and lived among us.

For all these blessings of the incarnation, God with us, we praise and give glory to you, as the grateful recipients of your grace and truth. You have not withheld your love from us, but have sent forth a light to shine in our darkness. You have destined us in love to your sons and daughters through Jesus Christ. For this we give you thanks and praise in the name of the child born in a stable in Bethlehem. Amen.

Jer. 31:7-14

John 1:1-14

God of Light, you bring hope to our world and joy to our lives. And yet we continue to be content in the shadows where less seems to be demanded of us. Dark depression and worried futures dim our faith. Anger and violence overpower gentle words. Despair casts a shadow of doubt on our hopes. Greed causes us to hold on to our gifts rather than sharing them with others. Racism and sexism keep us from receiving your light from one another.

We pray, O God, that you would open our eyes to the light of your star and open our hearts to the needs of others. Enable us to welcome the foreigner, to embrace the stranger and to share our abundance and wealth with those in need. Enable us to let the light of Christ lead and direct us.

We lift our prayers this day, O God of Hope, for those places in our world in need of your light of reconciliation, of forgiveness, of understanding. Our prayers are with our world leaders that they might find a light through the darkness. Help us to know that no amount of darkness can overcome the light that has come into our world. Grant that the peace that passes all understanding may settle upon all the nations of the world.

And so today, as the Magi did so long ago, we journey to the manger to offer our gifts and ourselves to the Christ child. We lay before the child the realities of our life, both good and bad. We offer our joy and love and laughter that they may be made holy. We relinquish our bitterness and hatred and worry, that we might be made whole once more.

Send the star to shine on us and lead us afresh to the embodiment of your love in the child of Bethlehem. For you have shown us, your pilgrim people, a glimpse of your kingdom of love and light. For this we give you thanks and recommit our lives to your purposes. Amen.

Isaiah 60:1-6

Matthew 2:1-12

Loving God, you have brought light into our darkness through your anointed one, Jesus of Nazareth. You have poured upon us the cleansing waters of new life and have sent your Spirit to guide and strengthen us in our journey. The former things have come to pass and we eagerly await the new things you shall bring forth. You have fulfilled your promises and chosen us to be your own.

Sometimes we feel overwhelmed by your grace and your love for us. It is not easy to love as you do. Sometimes we are too proud, sometimes too distracted, sometimes too apathetic, sometimes too hurt ourselves to really love others the way you love us. And so we entrust our lives to you in the spirit of our baptism. Renew our faith. Renew our unity. Renew our ministry to others.

For we seek to be your servants. Enable us to open the eyes that are blind. Enable us to bring out the prisoners from the darkness. Heal our minds, our bodies and our hearts, that we may go out from here today to bring your healing touch to all the broken and despondent peoples of the world. Give peace to the troubled, wholeness to the sick, companionship to the lonely, commitment to the fainthearted and hope to the broken in spirit.

O God, who has spoken to us through a baby born in Bethlehem, we pray this morning for the children of the world and for their future. Help us all to be participants in that future...a future that will be filled with promise, goodness, safety, dignity and hope. We especially lift prayers for the children baptized this morning and for their families. Send down your Spirit, loving God, to touch their lives and ours in such a way that we are infused with your power and sustained by your love. May we hear that still, small voice within us saying, "This is my beloved daughter, this my beloved son, with whom I am well pleased." Waters of life, call us, cleanse us, heal us and free us that your majesty may be made known throughout all the created world. Amen.

Isaiah 42:1-9

Matthew 3:13-17

ome Holy Spirit. We call on you to baptize us anew with your healing power and sustaining presence. In our times of trial, we long to hear your voice saying; "You are my son and daughter, the Beloved, with you I am well-pleased."

Sometimes we don't feel beloved. Circumstances in our lives, past or present, too often continue to have a heavy hold on us, making us feel inadequate and unworthy of the great gift of your love. But even in our times of sadness, despair, grief or uncertainty, you are present calling us by name, coaxing us to new life, working through many people and experiences to awaken our hearts to receive your spirit.

Today we rejoice because just as we remember the baptism of our Lord, we are called to claim that same promise of new birth through the waters of renewal and regeneration. We especially lift up those children who will receive the sacrament of baptism this morning. Through the water and the laying on of hands to invoke the Holy Spirit, may your newly adopted children learn to speak with your voice, touch with your hands, and love with your heart.

We also pray that you would help each of us to feel that we are your beloved children, uniquely special in our own way and precious in your sight. Enable us to know in our hearts that nothing we have done in the past, or will do in the future, can cause you to abandon us. Teach us that our value is measured by how much we are loved by you, not by the sum of our accomplishments. As Jesus was sent forth for his mission in this world through his baptism and empowerment by the Holy Spirit, may we leave this place this morning convinced of our own worth and able to help convince others of their priceless worth in your sight. Amen.

Acts 8:14-17

Luke 3:15-17; 21-22

Creator God, we are especially thankful this morning for this season of new beginnings. In this season of Epiphany, we celebrate the beginning of the ministry of Jesus Christ. And in baptism, we are witnesses to your presence and grace as your holy people whom you have called by name.

We give thanks for the water of life. We recall the splash of a baby's bath, the crash of waves on an ocean floor, the gentle, falling rain that nourishes our parched soil, the tear in a friend's eye, the delicate dew, and the early morning frost. Your living water brings renewal to our dry and empty lives. Your living water replenishes us so that we are once again able to pour ourselves out for others. Your living water restores us for the journey yet to come. Your living water reminds us of who we are.

Even as your son becomes a beacon of light and hope in our darkness, we are all too aware, O God, that there are many people still living in darkness. May we be empowered in ministry to carry your light and hope into the world. In that spirit we lift our prayers to you.

For the peace of the world and the unity of all peoples, we lift our prayers.

For the good earth which you have given us and for the wisdom and will to conserve it, we lift our prayers.

For the poor and oppressed, for the unemployed and the destitute, for prisoners and captives, we lift our prayers.

For those struggling with illness and for those who grieve the loss of a loved one, we lift our prayers.

For the leaders of nations that there may be justice and peace on earth, we lift our prayers.

For your church, for the priesthood of all believers and for this church that seeks to be in mission to others, we lift our prayers.

And so, Creator God, pour out your Holy Spirit on us this day. As we go out into the world, may the wetness of water nourish our dreams, may the coolness ease our burdens and may the loving touch of your Spirit bring us all into your tender care and embrace. May we celebrate your new creation all around us every moment of every day. Amen.

Matthew 3:11-17

ivine Spirit, you have bestowed upon each of us such a variety of gifts. The abundance of your many blessings and your goodness fill us with gratitude and joy. And yet we sometimes think our hour has not come. We hold back from sharing from our abundance, out of fear, doubt, envy, and mistrust. At other times we get caught up in our own hard times and we close ourselves off to the possibilities of new life that you continually make available to us. It is your living water that strengthens us in our times of hardship. It is your life-giving presence that enlivens us when our joy has run dry like wine that has been consumed by too many demands on our lives.

At times like these, we pray that you would transform our grumbling and complaints into fine wine. For just as your Son graced the wedding at Cana, may we open our hearts to invite the Christ to fill the empty spaces in our lives with a renewed sense of joy in life.

This church, in particular, O God, has been the recipient of so many gifts and has much to celebrate. Each person adds to the richness of the wine which we in turn serve to others as a church in mission. Enable us to be infused with compassion that we might hear and respond to the unspoken cries of your children in need of healing of mind, body or spirit. Enable us to be instruments of your hope to those who have lost their way, instruments of your grace to those who need to begin again, and instruments of your love to the lonely and forgotten ones. Enable us to celebrate with exuberance and joy the many opportunities and possibilities you set before us like a bountiful feast. Enable us to make your love a reality in this world, for all we have comes from one source, your great love for us. And so we humbly offer all of our gifts and all of ourselves to your glory. Amen.

1 Cor. 12:1-11

John 2:1-12

We come together this morning, aware and open to the new light that you have given us in Jesus Christ. We come together to refocus our priorities and to become more alert to your action in our lives. We come together to find new joy in all the ways you have blessed us. And we come together seeking your direction in ways that we might break down the barriers we have created among ourselves, and against you, so that others may be drawn to your lifesaving love. Finally, we come to hear again the summons of Jesus, "Follow me!" We ask that we might be led in ways where we might proclaim the gospel of your realm in our daily living. We recommit to you all of ourselves-our devotion, our time, our talents, our commitment to faithful service.

For you bring light into our darkness. You increase our joy. You ease our burdens. And so, in faith, we set those burdens before you that you might lighten the yoke upon our shoulders.

We place before you our fragmented busy lives. Teach us that we need not depend on our doing and having for our sense of worth. In your mercy, Lord, hear our prayers.

We place before you our friends-the hurt, the addicted, the sorrowing, the struggling child, the frustrated parent, the fragile marriage. Teach us the sacrament of care as we reach out to others in acts of love. In your mercy, Lord, hear our prayers.

We place before you our church. Teach us the way of trust and compassion and empower us to share the story of our faith where we live and work. In your mercy, Lord, hear our prayers.

We place before you our broken world, a world yearning for justice and freedom. Teach us the paths of peace and give us a brighter vision and hope for the future. In your mercy, Lord, hear our prayers.

And so, Loving God, we open ourselves this day to your ceaseless outpouring of love. We awake each day to your presence. When we are anxious or troubled, you comfort us. When we are faced with difficult choices that confuse us, you are there to guide us. You have surrounded us with your love before we even turned to you. May we in turn follow you as faithful disciples our whole life long. Amen.

Isaiah 9:1-4   Matthew 4:12-23

Loving God, all of life is a call and a response. You continually call us into new life and new beginnings. You call us from complacency to action, and sometimes that feels scary to us. Your call is often a call to change...a call to transform the old into something new...a call to stand up for those things that bring dignity and respect to all your children.

Sometimes you call us to make changes in our personal lives. You ask each of us to look at our values, our prejudices and those places in our lives in need of healing. At other times you call us to follow you, and to bring your world into a world that is fractured, divided and hurting. You call us to join together in community, as your church, to be a light of hope in this city and to the people we serve.

Yes, your call is a challenge and we may have to re-evaluate old ways of thinking. You challenge us to face our prejudices and our fears and to become instruments of positive change in the world. And while we may be uncomfortable with parts of your call and your challenge to us, help us to answer in faith as Moses did, saying, "Here I Am." Help us to leave behind our nets as did those early disciples and to trust that you will guide us into the future.

We have many areas of our life in need of prayer, and so we bring these concerns of our hearts to you in prayer, Loving God, knowing that you work for the good in all things.

We lift prayers for those who are sick and in need of your healing touch, for those who grieve and are in need of your comfort, and for those who have lost their way and are in need of your guidance. In your mercy, Lord, hear our prayers.

We lift prayers for all persons with physical and emotional challenges. Help us to realize that in your Kingdom, the only blind eyes are the ones that refuse to see with the heart, the only deaf ears are the ones that cannot hear with compassion, and the only paralyzed limbs are the ones weighed down by prejudice and fear. In your mercy, Lord, hear our prayers.

O God of Change, Invitation and Challenge, let us hear your word to us this day. Divert our attention from those things that divide and misdirect our commitment. Release us, that we may receive your spirit. Transform us and we shall know a world transformed. Amen.

Exodus 3:1-12   Mark 1:14-20

Some of us come this morning needing to be empowered by your Spirit. We need to be anointed by the Holy Spirit to face the tasks and challenges set before us. Just as Jesus was tempted, so too, are we tempted to misuse the power and authority you bestow on us. We are tempted to find our self-identity, our value, our meaning and purpose in life, through the deeds we do or do not do and by the tasks we perform or do not perform.

Help us, O God, to understand that you love and accept us as we are. Even when we give in to the many temptations around us, it is your word that leads us home. We do not live by bread alone, but by every word which comes forth from your mouth. Enable us to hear your unique word to us this evening. Empower us by your Word to be compassionate and caring persons even as we lift our prayers for those who are sick, those who hunger and thirst, those with no place to call home, those who are alienated and in need of your forgiveness and healing. We come to this table just as we are. Receive us, renew us, love us, O God, just as we are. In the name of Christ we pray. Amen.

Matthew 3:16 - 4:4

Loving God, we marvel at your majesty and power. You make your presence known to us in so many ways if only we could have eyes to see, ears to hear and hearts to comprehend. Just as Jesus astonished the people of Galilee with his teachings and the miracle of his healing grace, so you work in the ordinary of our daily living, surprising us with joy and empowering us to move through the difficult times in our lives. For this we give you thanks.

We give thanks today, O God, that your presence is felt even in the midst of tragedy. Your healing grace is present as neighbor helps neighbor, as communities gather together to bring relief and as we are given the opportunity, once again, to minister to those in need.

We give thanks for the birth of babies, for the laughter of children, for young people finding purpose and direction, for doors that are opened and for dreams that become reality. Help us to know that even when we are forced to confront change against our will, whether it be through natural disaster, divorce, illness, loss of a job or the death of a loved one, you guide us through the difficult times. You enable us to emerge as new and better persons. Our times of questioning and confusion are times that we are humbled in your presence. As we let go of the old, we are opened to the new. We are given the chance to grow in faith and to make the adjustments needed in our lives. A time of change, chaos, and breaking down, becomes an opportunity to build anew; and for this we give you thanks.

And so, Divine Spirit, enable us to respond to your call to be a prophetic witness in our words and deeds. Out of our own need for renewal and clearer vision, we are here to remember that, in all circumstances, we are loved and accepted unconditionally by you. In Christ we experience healing and wholeness and dare to reach out to help others. Amen.

Mark 1:21-28

We come before you, O God, on this day when we acknowledge and celebrate our love for one another and our love for you. You sent your son Jesus who taught us the meaning of love and for this we give you thanks. And yet we must confess that we don't always act out of love. We are often quick to anger, to want justice our way, to let our accusations fly. You know our thoughts. Not only do you see the actions of our hands, but you know the motives of our hearts. You know when our anger is justified and maybe even necessary. But when anger's time is through, help us to see through our anger to a love and a peace that surpasses all understanding. Help us to move to a place of healing and wholeness. Help us to choose the way of life and to hold fast to the commandments you have given us.

Yes, Divine Spirit, we come before you on this day when we acknowledge and celebrate our love for one another and our love for you. It is in that spirit of love that we lift our prayers of intercession.

We remember the poor, and ask that we may find ways to feed them; and the sick, that they may receive healing. In your mercy, Lord, hear our prayers.

We pray for the grieving that their hearts may be comforted; for the lonely that they might find relationship and for the fearful that they may be given confidence. In your mercy, Lord, hear our prayers.

We lift prayers for the doubtful, that they may have faith; for the cynical, that they may experience trust; and for all children and young people, that they may be kept from harmful ways. In your mercy, Lord, hear our prayers.

We pray for ourselves that we might follow you in faithfulness all the days of our lives. We especially pray this day for someone with whom we are angry or a situation that calls for healing and reconciliation. At this time, we lift that name to you. In your mercy, Lord, hear our prayers.

You have set before us this day life and death, blessing and curse, good and evil. Help us to choose life that we might live. Deepen our compassion for others, O God. Stir up our commitment. Help us to live this day and throughout the year as children of the covenant, created, called out and commissioned by the one whose name is above every name, even Jesus our Lord. Amen.

Deut. 30:15-20   *Matthew 5:21-27*

So often, Divine Spirit, we feel as if we are abiding in the parched places of our personal wildernesses. We long to be like trees planted by streams of water, sending out roots to all we can touch, and yielding fruit in season. But our fears, our anxieties and our doubts hold us back from becoming the people we would like to be.

Yet, in spite of our shortcomings, you are a blessing God. You promise healing to all who trust in your power. You promise realms of heaven to the poor, food to the hungry, joy to those who weep, and acceptance to the forsaken. You inspire us to embrace high standards in our daily living and to seek those values which enhance life rather than destroy life.

Yes, there are times, Loving Creator, when we need to be reminded of your promises to us. We need to be reminded that you created us and formed us and that you call each one of us by name. You have claimed us as your children. We are your own. We are precious in your sight. For your promises and many blessings, we lift our praise, our thanksgiving and our prayers.

In you alone we place our trust. Fill us with your loving presence. God of Mercy, hold us in love.

Grant us patience in all that we endure, that we may follow you more closely. God of Mercy, hold us in love.

Give heart to those who are low in spirit. Look upon the tears of the poor. God of Mercy, hold us in love.

Teach us to bear one another's burdens and so fulfill your law of love. God of Mercy, hold us in love.

Send your Holy Spirit upon your Church. Guide and uphold all who you claim as your people. God of Mercy, hold us in love.

Renew our hearts in dedication to your will. Send your Spirit to all of your children. God of Mercy, hold us in love.

As your children we are renewed, restored and refreshed to go into the world to be witnesses to your love and presence in our lives. We go into the world to bring your healing touch to others and to share in your abiding love...a love which has endured throughout the ages. Amen.

Jeremiah 17:5-10   Luke 6:17-26

verlasting God, we come to you this day amidst all the confusion of our lives and our world. We feel caught in the middle between those personal struggles that touch our lives so deeply and the greater struggle that has engaged our nation and our world. Sometimes we feel like we are fighting spirits, both those around us and those inside us.

And yet, in the midst of our struggles, Loving God, you provide prophetic voices arising among your people. You give us a vision of the future that is larger than our narrow sight. Just as Jesus astonished the people of Galilee with his teachings and the miracle of his healing power, so you work among us today, surprising us with hope and joy. With Jesus comes the word that is stronger than evil-the word that gives and restores life. And so, as grateful recipients of your love and grace, we once again lift our prayers to you.

We lift our prayers this day for all the nations of our world that they might be guided in the ways that lead to justice and peace.

We lift our prayers for those most closely touched by war and for the innocent victims of violence and oppression.

We lift our prayers for our earth, that all of us might treat your creation with reverence and care.

We pray for comfort and healing for those among us who suffer in mind, body or spirit. Give them courage and hope in their troubles and a vision of hope for the future.

We pray for the mission of this church that each of us might be faithful witnesses and agents of your healing love beyond the walls of this building.

And we lift prayers for ourselves, for the forgiveness of all our shortcomings, known and unknown, for those things we have done and those we have left undone. Enable us to begin again to serve you in newness of life. Amen.

Deut. 18:15-20   Mark 1:21-28

oving God, we seek to be faithful followers, but we are all too aware of our human frailty and weakness. You ask a lot of us. You call us to love our enemies. You call us to respond to hurt and betrayal with forgiveness. We confess that your ways are not easy ones for us. It is difficult to be like Joseph, who embraced and wept with his brothers who had sought to destroy him. It is not easy to reconcile with those who hurt us or to forgive those who have abused us in some way. It is hard when trust is broken.

In this time of prayer, O God, we ask for your forgiveness even as we seek to forgive others. Forgive us when we have cursed those who have cursed us. Forgive us for the times we have lashed out in bitterness and anger. Forgive us when we break down relationships rather than seeking to bring about healing and wholeness. Forgive us when our own ego and pride get in the way and we judge others without knowing their story or perspective.

Trusting in your grace and unconditional love, we lift our prayers to you this morning. We lift prayers for those who struggle with addictions of all kinds, for the innocent victims of violence and oppression, and for those for whom doubt, despair and fear are daily companions. In your mercy, Lord, hear our prayers.

We pray for comfort and healing for those among us who suffer in mind, body or spirit. Give us courage and hope in our troubles and a vision of hope for the future. In your mercy, Lord, hear our prayers.

We pray for all families, but especially families where there is strife and brokenness. We ask especially that you give strength to single parents, to the children of divorce and to families who struggle with challenges and adversities of all kinds. In your mercy, Lord, hear our prayers.

We lift prayers for someone for whom we feel anger and resentment even as we name that person in our heart. Help us to find the path to reconciliation and forgiveness. In your mercy, Lord, hear our prayers.

We lift prayers for ourselves also, for the forgiveness of all our shortcomings, known and unknown, for those things we have done and those we have left undone, for closing you out at the times we need you most. Enable us to begin again to serve you in newness of life. In your mercy, Lord, hear our prayers.

Luke 6:27-38

So many times, O God, we come into your presence with our questions. Why is this happening to me? Why am I going through this? How can I help a loved one? We even ask where you are, O God, and what you are doing in times of our uncertainty, our pain, our despair, our helplessness.

Yet it is you who promises to comfort us in all our afflictions. You comfort us, Healing Spirit, that we might console others. Just as you instructed your prophet Isaiah to "Comfort, O Comfort my people", we too are called to be instruments of your healing and grace in this broken world.

And so, assured of your mercies and consolations toward us, we lift our prayers in confidence and in thanksgiving for your ever present love. For as you share in our sufferings, O God, so also do you share in our healing. As grateful recipients of your promises, we lift our prayers to you.

We pray for peace between nations and for peace between all your children. Where there is blindness to your righteousness, may we dare to share visions of a just and compassionate world. O Lord, hear us we pray. O Lord, hold us in your love.

We pray for ourselves and our loved ones that you would watch over us and keep us from danger and temptation. O Lord, hear us we pray. O Lord, hold us in your love.

We pray for a renewed sense of faith and trust in your grace. O Lord, hear us we pray. O Lord, hold us in your love.

For all your blessings, O God, we give you thanks and renew our covenant that you shall be our God and we shall be your people. For you make new in us a faith, that no matter what we face, we can be assured of your promise of new life and new beginnings through Jesus Christ, our Lord. Amen.

Isaiah 40:1-5

God, we confess that we are the ones who are poor in spirit. We are the ones who mourn the losses in our lives. We are the ones who hunger and thirst for justice and truth in our world. You offer blessings to us in our yearnings, and yet we often miss your loving presence. We get caught up in our own circumstances and at times we question where the blessing can be in the midst of all the despair, sadness, emptiness, and anxiety that we feel inside and see all around us. Yet we yearn for you still.

Have mercy upon us, O God. Lead us beyond our weaknesses. Lift us above our doubts and help us to see the healing and forgiveness you continually make available to us. Help us to have strength in the midst of our struggles and to be open enough to receive your blessings.

As recipients of your blessing love and grace we are called to share your blessings with all your children. And so we lift our prayers for ourselves and on behalf of others.

We pray for all who are heavy burdened. We pray especially for those who have lost jobs or are worried about employment. Gently bind their wounds. In your mercy, Lord, hear our prayers.

Renew our hearts in dedication to your will. Send your spirit upon all of your children who are hurting or in special need. In your mercy, Lord, hear our prayers.

We give thanks for your presence in all the created world. May we find you in the sorrowing and the poor. In your mercy, Lord, hear our prayers.

Empower us to be a light of the world and the salt of the earth. In your mercy Lord, hear our prayers.

Look with favor on all who trust in your grace and love. Fill each of us with the blessing of mind, body and spirit. In your mercy, Lord, hear our prayers.

Gentle Spirit, help us to be patient and to take time to find you in our everyday lives. Help us to look to the ordinary to find your blessing in lost coins, in widow's mites, in mustard seeds. Help us to find the holy in relationships healed, in hope restored, in the chance to begin again. You are a holy and wondrous God, ready to satisfy the yearnings of our hearts if only we would be silent and listen for your voice. We have been drawn together to this place and time in the name of Christ and we give you thanks for your renewing presence. Amen.

We come before you today, O God, as grateful recipients of the many blessings you have bestowed upon us. It is we, your children, who are poor in spirit, who mourn and who hunger and thirst for justice. It is we who carry with us the private burdens of sickness, trouble and grief. It is we who carry with us the shared burdens of our involvement with injustice, oppression and violence in whatever forms they may be manifested.

And yet, O God, you continue to bestow blessings upon us. It is your grace that saves us from ourselves, heals our brokenness and brings life out of our deaths. It is your grace that causes us to re-evaluate who we are, what our values are and where our commitments need to be. It is your grace that enables us to see beyond what the world is, to a vision of what the world can be.

And so, in response to your many blessings and obedience to the teachings of Jesus, we are called once again to respond. We are called to share our blessings with others both as individuals and as communities of faith. Help us to embrace opportunities and moments to make a difference in Christ's name. Empower us, we pray, to go into the world doing what you require...bringing justice where we can, loving kindness, and humbly walking the path set before us. Touch us with your grace as we recommit ourselves this day to a faithful life. Amen.

Matthew 5:1-12

Creator God, we bring to this time of prayer so many needs and concerns. We bring our hurts and our loneliness, our grief and our fears, our broken relationships and our anxiety about the future. And often, O God, we come to these times of prayer with our preconceived ideas of how you can make things right again. We like to be in control and we come to you hoping that you will fix things in a certain way so that we can go on as before.

And yet by setting your agenda, O God, we limit you so. Often we miss the surprising new opportunities and the unthought-of possibilities for healing and for growth that you may be offering to us.

So we ask you, Divine Spirit, to help us to be open to those new possibilities and those unpredictable surprises. Help us to celebrate and embrace the many ways that you choose to begin healing, hope and wholeness back into our lives. We pray for your healing to take place in our lives...in those quiet, hidden places of our minds, with our physical bodies, in our relationships with family and friends, and in our places of work and play.

Let the love and power that were in Jesus Christ envelop us and empower us that we might let our healing power flow out from us to a sick and hurting world, that politicians might govern with compassion, that world rulers might be safe in their homes, and that little children might grow up in a world of joy, expectation and wonder.

Just as Jesus began his ministry by healing others, so we are called to go out into the world to carry your message of healing and of hope to all of creation. Amen.

Mark 1:40-45

racious God, you show your love for us in so many ways. When things seem the bleakest and the darkest, you break into our lives in surprising and unexpected ways. When we are trembling and afraid like Abraham, you make covenant with us and promise to be continually beside us. When we are sorrowing, you are there to gather us together as a hen gathers her brood under her wings. When we are doubting or have lost courage, you send your Word into our midst to show us the way. When we are called to make major changes in our lives, you are there to lead us to the promised land. When we waver in our commitments and discipleship, your steadfast love becomes our promise and our hope.

Keep us faithful, O God. In this season of Lent we are all too aware of our failings and shortcomings. Help us to follow the example of your prophets who showed us the way to a covenant relationship with you. In our hearts we desire to be faithful followers of your Son all the way to the cross. We desire to join the many faithful pilgrims who have traveled the road before us, for we are so thankful to be numbered among your sons and daughters. Through Christ you have called us and named us. And now, by your Spirit, empower and strengthen us for all that lies ahead. Show us the discipline of true discipleship. Give us the determination in this season to set aside time for prayer and quiet communion with you. In all the pressures and demands of our daily living, show us the power of silence that we might hear your word to us.

God of Tenderness and Strength, help us to see where love and hope and faith and healing are needed. We lift prayers for all those who suffer; the malnourished and the starving, the victims of violence, the victims of natural disasters, the victims of AIDS. We pray for those who are ill, especially the persons we name in our hearts. We pray for those who are disabled, who seek fulfillment, understanding, dignity and self-worth. We pray for those distressed in mind and spirit; the bereaved, the anxious, the unemployed, those who are hurt or afraid. Show us how we might work in our world, right where we are, to bring healing and wholeness into the lives of nations, of communities, of families and of individuals. For it is your Son who first showed us the power of compassion and unconditional love. Blessed is the one who comes in the name of the Lord. Amen.

Gen. 15:1-12;17,18   *Luke 13:31-35*

God, source of all grace and mercy, we come before you this day with all our limitations, fears, doubts and personal deaths. We've been told, and we believe, that beyond every death, large or small, there is resurrection and new life. And yet, O God, we often find ourselves fearing life itself more than we fear death in its many forms. To receive life requires us to change...to let go...to entrust ourselves to your transforming love. New life can be demanding...even threatening. And so we cling to familiar patterns and ways. We cling to illusions of life, rather than risking change...rather than losing our life in order to receive life.

We pray today, O God, source of all grace and mercy, that you would open the tombs of our souls. Enable us to let go of the illusion that we are in control of our own lives...an illusion that brings fear instead of hope, isolation instead of community, death instead of life. You know our many needs this day, our hurts, our disappointments, our grief, our anxiety. You also know that in the midst of life events that trouble us so, there are also those events in our lives which fill us with joy and thanksgiving. We give thanks for love newly found, for health restored, for opportunities provided, for the gift of friendship, for the birth of babies. You have blessed us in many ways and we pray that our lives might, in turn, be a blessing to others.

Help us to truly be instruments of your peace in this world so in need of healing and reconciling love. Help us bring your hope to those who suffer in mind, body or spirit. Help us to bring your forgiveness to those who feel caught in the web of past failures and regrets. Help us to take up our cross, to follow Jesus, and to work toward the day when all your creation will move out of the desert into your promised land, from death to life abundant. Amen.

Mark 8:31-38

We seek your special presence today, O God, as we move into this Lenten journey that will lead us to the cross. We pray that you would minister to us in our personal wildernesses as you ministered to Jesus in his times of testing and temptation. You alone know when we are troubled, confused, and have lost our way. You alone know when we face the difficult times of temptation.

In this season of Lent, you call us to personal and corporate penitence, accountability, and preparation. Loving God, as you strengthened Jesus to choose rightly when he was tempted in the wilderness, so strengthen us, through your presence and Spirit, that when we face temptation, we may be given the vision and courage to make the right choices. Help us to recognize and turn away from those forces that lead us away from life abundant.

When we follow the voices of crowds instead of seeking your guidance and your will, grant us your grace, O God, and set us free.

When we are too quick to judge others without first looking at ourselves, grant us your grace, O God, and set us free.

When we respond to human need and suffering with apathy and to injustice and cruelty with indifference, grant us your grace, O God, and set us free.

When we waste and pollute this world which you have created, grant us your grace, O God, and set us free.

When our love of worldly goods and comforts blinds us to the needs of others, grant us your grace, O God, and set us free.

Grant us your grace, O God. Heal our pain, remove our doubt, forgive our failures. Help us to accept your love and forgiveness, so that we might be set free in grace to follow you and to serve you. We lift these prayers in the name of your Son and our Savior, Jesus Christ. Amen.

Matthew 4:1-11

Loving God, sometimes we feel like a wilderness people, stumbling along, scrounging for food to nourish our souls, searching for living water. Too often we put our faith and trust in the pursuit of worldly values instead of placing trust in you to fill our needs, to accompany us on the journey and to challenge us to live a faithful life.

In this season of Lent, O God, we examine our lives and recognize our need to repent. We need to do an about face on those habits, addictions, and behaviors that keep us from bearing fruit and sharing with others the spiritual gifts you have bestowed upon us. You know where we have slipped and fallen. You know the areas in which we are especially vulnerable to temptation. And so we pray that you would sustain us in our journey through Lent and give us the willingness to do the loving thing and to be faithful in the small acts of caring for others.

Show us how we might bring hope, harmony, and love into our battered and bruised world. We lift prayers for those who struggle with sickness of mind, body, and spirit, and pray that they may be surrounded by persons who can assure them of your constant love and presence. We lift prayers for those who have suffered losses, whether it be a loved one, a job, a relationship, or, most importantly, a loss of confidence. Direct their paths in the way that leads to meaningful direction and hope for the future. We pray that you would ease our own fears and our sorrows, our storms and our clouds, our doubts and our complacency.

Holy God, journey with us this Lenten season that we might discover the hidden spring in every wilderness. Help us to live the unanswered questions and doubts of our soul, knowing that, in time, you will open to us a deeper awareness of your truth and love. God of living water and promised resurrection, work your surprising and amazing grace in our lives and in our broken world. Amen.

Isaiah 55:1-9   Luke 13:1-9

Shepherd God, we come to you in this time of quiet gathering, ever thankful that you lovingly lead us beside still waters. Sometimes we feel that our lives are in such turmoil and confusion. We long to lie down in green pastures. We come needing to be restored. And yet we confess that it isn't always easy to follow your shepherding. It isn't always easy to allow ourselves to be led when we are so used to doing the leading.

Restore our trust and faith, O God, as you restore our souls. Lead us along the paths of righteousness and give us the clarity of vision to discern the way we should go. Like the blind man, we come today seeking the way out of our personal darkness. Let us feel the touch of clay upon our eyes that we might be healed of all the blindness that holds us back and limits our lives. Let your light illumine the dark places in our lives that we might see ourselves as you see us and that we might envision our future with hope. Enable us to live as children of the light even as we lift our prayers to you.

We lift prayers for our world, for peace among nations and justice for all your children. We lift prayers for our country and its leaders, that they might govern with compassion and understanding. We lift prayers for those people we know and for those who remain unnamed to us. May the lonely find fellowship, the grief-stricken find comfort, the homeless find shelter, the ill find healing, the angry find inner peace, and the alienated be brought back into community.

The issues that we face in our world often do not lend themselves to simple solutions. May your rod and staff comfort us with the promise of your love and your presence in all the times of our lives. As we pass through our personal valleys, may we be led by your light and refreshed by the promise that you shepherd us still. Amen.

Psalm 23   John 9:1-7, 18-25

ender God, you are our shepherd in times of trouble. When we tiptoe into the valley of the shadow of death, you are with us. When we find ourselves moving in new directions, into new pastures, you are there to guide us. When we are blind to seeing the simple acts of care and love that would make such a difference to another, you open our eyes.

We confess, O God, that we often refuse to heed your call. We want to go our own way...to trust in our own efforts. And so, we refuse to be guided to the sources of nourishment and rest, the still waters, that you provide. We continue to carry around the burden of our poor choices rather than trusting in your forgiveness and grace. We respond to pressing human need with fear and pain and inaction. We hide our anxieties, our fears, our resentments, and our self-centeredness, even from you.

And so, Great Shepherd, seek us out. Watch over us. Draw us unto yourself. We give you thanks for sending your Son, Jesus, who shows us the way to trust and to follow. Just as Jesus showed himself to be the light of the world, enable us to be reflections of that light. Even as Jesus shows us the way to healing and wholeness, enable us to become whole persons as we learn to trust in your presence, your love and your guidance. Lead us by your Spirit to grow in wisdom and understanding of what it means to be the sheep of your pasture. Amen.

Psalm 23

God, we confess that it is not easy to follow Jesus on this Lenten journey to the cross. We are reluctant to come face to face with our own human needs, our own fears, our own pain, and our own inaction in the face of suffering. And yet we find that the cross of Jesus becomes a place where we judge both our individual lives and our world.

We are reluctant to give up and leave behind a past way of life or point of view that has become comfortable for us. We try to find our security in such things as material possessions, money, social status, educational degrees or religious pedigrees. We are not so different, O God, from those persons so long ago who led our Lord to the cross. Even today people are crucified by those same forces that destroyed Jesus.

Help us to understand, Loving God, that in Christ we already have all that we need to possess. Help us to understand that our real hope for new life and new beginnings begins with our faith and trust in you. Walk with us to the cross. Hold us up as we stumble and fall. Anoint us with your love and grace so that we might become an extension of your love to all we meet in the journey. Anoint us and prepare us to speak that kind word, to give the gift of our presence, to extend that helping hand to our neighbor in need, to embrace one another across lines of difference.

Continue to walk with us to the cross, O God, for in your presence we find light in our darkness, strength in our weakness, joy in our tears and new life out of death. For this we give thanks as we rededicate ourselves to accepting the cost and joy of discipleship to Jesus Christ, our faithful guide. Amen.

oving God, how we yearn for you. Deep inside we desire to know that you love and accept us just as we are. We seek release from our past mistakes and regrets and the opportunity to move beyond the hurt and pain of our lives. We look for direction, for signs, for your leadings and guidance for the important decisions we are faced with each day. Yes, we yearn to really know you, for you are our God and we are your people.

As we draw closer to the cross in this Lenten season, we, like the disciples and others, seek to understand the mystery of Christ who draws all people to Himself. Lent offers us the space to explore those dry places inside, the rocky ground, the turbulent waters, and to discover anew the wellspring of your constant love. We need the reassurance that you are present with us in our dark and difficult times, knowing that you do not abandon us in our time of need. We need to learn to trust in your presence, to live the unanswered questions in our hearts, and to wait in the darkness knowing that your transforming power is ever working in our lives. Help us to wait in trust that you can redeem all seemingly hopeless situations in our lives and our world.

You hold us in your loving arms in our times of trial. You embrace us even in the times when we are forced to die to old ways of living. In your mercy, we lift to your care and protection all those who face illness this day, all those who grieve some loss in their lives, all those who struggle with addiction, all those who have lost a sense a purpose, meaning and hope, all those who are the victims of abuse, injustice, and oppression of all kinds. Cleanse our hearts this day. Awaken our spirits. Restore in us the joy of living life fully and abundantly. Amen.

Jer. 31:31-34   *John 12:20-33*

Creator God, sometimes it feels like our dreams have dried up and our hopes are lost. We sometimes feel that your Spirit, which blows where it will, has passed us by. We have become dry bones. Something in us, which we cannot name, has died, and like Lazarus, we lie bound in the dark and cold of our personal tomb.

We confess, O God, that we often find ourselves in such a predicament because we have not been receptive to your presence. We ignore the winds of your Spirit and the light of your promise to be with us in all the times of our lives. We become unloved and unloving, like lifeless dry bones strewn in the desert. In these times, you weep over us, as Jesus wept with compassion for Lazarus, yearning to draw us back to your endless stream of love and mercy.

And so this morning, we seek to be open to your presence and to be receptive to your Spirit that dwells in our midst, for you, O God, create life, overcome darkness, and conquer death. We know this in our hearts, but sometimes we can't comprehend what that means for our lives at this moment. Violent events in the world frighten us. The magnitude of problems weakens our resolve to take positive action for constructive change.

Yet we want to be made new. And so give us hearts of courage that we may not hide from those who suffer, but rather walk up to their tombs and call out for new life. Give us strength to walk with, and if need be, to hold up those among us who are wounded by grief, illness, broken relationships, depression, unemployment, or simply a sense of having lost their way. Our souls rest in you, in the promise of new possibilities, and in the newness of life which you continually make available to us. Amen.

Ezekial 37:1-6;11-14   *John 11:17-45*

Redeeming God, your Son has graced our lives with a priceless gift beyond all measure. Christ has poured out his spirit in compassion for us. Such a gift should inspire us to a ministry of caring for others that knows no barriers...no limits. But we confess, O God, that our response has hardly been so generous. We are cautious in love and careful about sharing our affection. There are those moments when we feel so blessed in our lives that we are tempted to do something extravagant as the woman at Bethany did when she anointed Jesus with costly nard. But we squelch those impulses, afraid of appearing foolish, preferring not to stand out from the crowds and risk ridicule.

Grant us endurance, Indwelling God, to persevere in faith and in our journey when the acclaim has ceased, when the voices of the crowd are still, when the joyful hosannas are replaced with the darkness and emptiness of our souls. When we face fears and betrayals, grant us faith, we pray, to still walk toward your promise. When we are overcome by trials and suffering, and want to turn back, grant us courage to continue the journey. By following Jesus we will discover that your grace is stronger than any of the powers that would hold us back; meet us in the midst of our brokenness and our unfaithfulness where we await your healing presence. We entrust ourselves once again to your unfailing love and grace. Amen.

Mark 14:3-9

Palm Sunday

osanna in the highest. Blessed is he who comes in the name of the Lord. How we love a parade! We eagerly line the streets and fill the sanctuaries to witness the triumphant entrance of Jesus into the city and into our lives. We get caught up in the excitement of the crowd and of this season. We anticipate the victory over the forces of death that we know to be part of the Easter season of new life and new beginnings. But when the crowds have all gone home, we shrink back into our comfortable lives seeking to avoid the difficult journey that we know lies ahead. We push aside the Maundy Thursdays and the Good Fridays of our lives because it is uncomfortable for us to face betrayal, suffering, and death. We confess, Divine Spirit, that we often move easily from the exuberance of Palm Sunday to the triumph of Easter. But apart from the crowds, we are forced to come face to face with our own questions, our own confusions, our own doubts, our own fears.

And so in the quiet of this time together, O God, we seek your presence in a special way. We seek the courage to walk with Jesus all the way to the cross. We seek your guidance and strength in facing the trials of our own lives and of those we love. Be with those whose energies are sapped by sorrow, whose bodies are bent with grief. Be with those who are scorned by their neighbors or who are cast aside as being inferior and of no more use. Be with those who suffer in mind, spirit, and body and give them a sense of hope and renewed purposes.

We seek to follow Christ and not betray Him. Help us to empty ourselves of false intentions and to open ourselves to your will as Christ did. Strengthen us for the betrayals and crucifixions we face, that our faith and love may bring us victory over all that would bring us down. Teach us by Christ's example that when darkness and difficulty come over us, we gather our best friends around us and share our love without restraint. In sharing with others, we are in turn healed and made whole. Open us to the depths of your love hidden in the mystery of this week. Let us feel your presence and forgiveness even when we betray, deny, and run away. Walk with us, Sustaining God, and lead us from denial to affirmation and from death to life. Amen.

Mark 11:1-11

oving God, we want to follow you. But sometimes what you ask seems so hard. We are reluctant to take up our crosses for fear that they will be too heavy. We get uncomfortable with all this talk about losing our life in order to save our life. And it is difficult to grasp the meaning of suffering, rejection, and death as the path Jesus had to walk.

And yet we know that we learn something of who we are by discovering who Jesus is. We experience the paradox that the way to self-fulfillment is the way of self-denial. And we learn that faithful discipleship is what really gives meaning to our lives.

So in this time of quiet communion with you, O God, we lift our prayers. We lift prayers for those who are lonely and cry for companionship, for those who are sick and seek healing, for those who mourn and need to be comforted, for those who are confused and need direction, for those who are hungry and long to be fed, for those who are experiencing spiritual darkness and yearn for your light.

We pray that we may have the consciousness of Christ in our lives, that we might see others as you see them and that we might reach out in compassion to all of your children. We rejoice that your Spirit is within and around us this morning, empowering us to become your sons and daughters, filled with joy and truth. Amen.

Mark 8:31-38

God of Light, we come to you today seeking the gift of your light and your presence in our lives. Some of us prefer to linger in the shadows where we cannot see your light that tries to break into our lives. Others of us feel so isolated and alone that we cannot feel your nearness. Some of us are so weighted down by the knowledge of our faults and shortcomings, that we are separated from your promises and your love for us. And many of us have built walls that block out your healing light and your abiding compassion. And so we pray to you, O God of Light, that you would touch us where we are, that you would accept the unanswered questions in our hearts. Shepherd us beyond our hurts, beyond our fears, from death to life.

We are also filled with praise and thanksgiving this day. We give thanks for the waters of rain that refresh, replenish, and renew our earth and our souls. We give thanks for the gift of family, of friends and for this community in Christ that provides support, love, and guidance. We thank you for the gift of new opportunities, new possibilities, and new chances that you continually make available to us. But most of all, O God of Light, we thank you for sending your Son into our world and offering us the gift of your saving grace...a grace that frees us to act in the world in the sure and certain knowledge of your love for us. Let this Lenten season be for us a journey to clearness and direction. Send in your light and love to surround us, embrace us, and sustain us in all the seasons of our lives. Awaken our spirits and renew us to be your faithful disciples. Amen.

John 3:14-21   *Ephesians 2:4-10*

Wednesday in Holy Week

Saying good-bye is never easy. And yet at this time in our Lenten journey, O God, we are asked, along with the disciples, to say farewell to Jesus. His approaching has been announced, but are we ever ready to let go and face the reality of the painful times in our lives? We try to dismiss what we know in our hearts or use distractions and avoidance to pull us away from the pain we are asked to face. Even we, as followers of Jesus, are tempted at times to turn our heads, pretend we don't know what is going on, and so betray our faith and our discipleship. It is no wonder that we find our Lord troubled in spirit at this crucial time on his journey to the cross. Yes, Divine Spirit, we as followers of Jesus and as a community of faith, are in need of your love and grace as we continue our journey to the cross.

John 13:21-30

Maundy Thursday

Creator God, we come together tonight to keep your vigil at the cross. There are many other places where we could be. We would much rather be part of a celebration. On Palm Sunday we filled the sanctuary to witness the triumphant entrance of Jesus into the city of Jerusalem...and into our lives. We would much rather come together to celebrate the victory of Jesus on the cross. We could be filling Easter baskets, enjoying the signs of Spring, or shopping for new Easter clothes. We move so comfortably, O God, from Palm Sunday to Easter Sunday. But in doing so, we pass over the Thursdays and Fridays of our lives. In doing so, we pass over your presence at the cross.

And so tonight we come together to affirm your presence in suffering and death, as well as in blessing and life. We come together to reclaim Maundy Thursday and Good Friday and to recognize your presence in our suffering and defeat. We come together to hear the words of the Christ who transforms our suffering and defeat into new life and new possibility. We come together to remember the suffering that came after the palm branches and before the Easter lilies.

As we reflect on the seven last words of Jesus, open our hearts, O Lord, that we might discover for ourselves the meaning He gave to suffering. Enable us, we pray, to find the grace to say, "Unto thy hands I commit my spirit." Enable us to face the tragedies of our own lives and transform them into new hope, new life, and new beginnings. Be with us, Divine Spirit, as we say "yes" to the Christ, and let us go all the way to the cross...together. We pray, as we would live, in the name of the one whose power is shaped by the cross, Jesus, our Christ. Amen.

Maundy Thursday

God of Unending Love, we are filled with so many conflicting feelings as we gather together on this holy night. We come to share the story and to break the bread together and to experience our common life in the body of Christ. We come in a spirit of reflection and even wonder, for the mysteries of this night are so much more than we can ever comprehend. We come aware of our many shortcomings and our need for your healing love.

And so we gather in this place to lift our prayers to you. We gather to remember the suffering of Christ on our behalf, in the hope that we will be enabled to face the sorrows and tragedies of our own lives. God of Mercy, hold us in your love.

We gather to confess our failure to trust you. Grant us your grace that we may learn to live in affirmation and not denial. God of Mercy, hold us in your love.

We gather to ask for guidance that we might use all the gifts you have entrusted to us for the redemption of our community and our world. Enable us to reach out to one another in times of grief or illness, and to embrace one another across lines of difference. God of Mercy, hold us in your love.

We gather together seeking your presence as we encounter our own Cavalry of the spirit. Enable us to bless those who use us falsely and to, in all times, commit our spirits to you in faith and trust. God of Mercy, hold us in your love.

We gather as a community aware of the many ways we have broken covenant with you. We open our hearts anew in preparation to receive your gifts of forgiveness, reconciliation, and healing. God of Mercy, hold us in your love.

Draw us together in heart and purpose this night and let your spirit be upon us in power and grace, for this hour and evermore. Amen.

Mark 14:12-26

Good Friday

O God, we gather together once more at the foot of the cross. Our hearts are heavy. In the midst of life, we are surrounded by death: the death of hope, the death of innocence, the death of promises, the death of dreams, even the death of those we love. We are like the sheep who have gone astray. For we confess, O Lord, that we have turned to pursue our own way instead of following your leadings. And our hearts are heavy.

Yet your message to us through Jesus Christ is not death, but life: the life of the Spirit, the life of dreams, the life of faith, the life of love, the life of justice for all your children, life for the broken and rejected, life for the diseased and afflicted, life for those we love, life for us. Help us to see that in dying with Christ, dying to self, we are promised a new beginning.

And so as we huddle together at the foot of the cross, we ask that you not abandon us in our time of need and trial. Hold us close, Loving God, as we face our own shadows and questions, as we feel our own doubts and betrayals, as we know our own fears of suffering and pain. Hold us close so that we might find your grace stronger than our fears. Hold us close so we might look in our hearts and find your forgiveness. Hold us close as we move from the woundedness of life into the healing of Easter. Amen.

Good Friday

God, we admit that Good Friday is not easy for us. It is not a day of safe distances. The darkness descends. The taunts and jeers reach our ears. Denial emerges from unlikely places. And we aren't sure that we have the courage to go all the way to the cross. We need you, now more than ever, when we enter our own valleys of the shadow of death. When darkness descends upon our own lives, help us to wait in faith and in the knowledge that you are present in the darkness to bring about transformation and new life.

And so our hearts are heavy with the tragedy of this day as we keep our vigil at the cross. But we are also a people of hope, ever aware of the possibilities available to sustain us and move us. We share in the agony of Jesus' rejection and death, knowing how often we add to the pain. The story of Christ's passion and death mirrors for us much of our own weakness and sin. We all come here as men and women who have missed the mark and who are alienated from God and our neighbor. Forgive us our shortcomings, we pray, and restore us to the wholeness you intend for all creation. Give strength to our love, that where life struggles to prevail, we would bring your renewing spirit. We pray, as we would live, in the name of Jesus, our Savior and our Christ. Amen.

Easter Sunday

The women found the stone rolled away, O God. They found the tomb empty. They were perplexed, frightened, and confused. Yet they were given the news that Christ had risen. And they believed.

It's harder for us, Lord. After all, we live in a time of scientific evidence and proof. To believe is asking so much of us...and yet so little. For you continue to work miracles in our live in the hush before the morning dawn. You continue to roll away those stumbling stones and bring life to our dead ends. You continue to delight and surprise us with empty tombs and unexpected visits. The signs of new life are all around, but like the disciples, we treat this joy as an idle tale and we do not believe.

Awaken in us, Divine Spirit, the joy of this morning. Awaken in us the wonder and awe of discovering your presence in our midst. Free us from all that is dead. Loose us from the things which we need to leave behind, the wrappings and trappings of death that keep us from becoming the persons you would have us be. Roll away the stones of our doubt. Call us together as an Easter people whereby we can challenge despair with glowing hope and where we can live joyfully and confidently even in the midst of the harsh realities of life.

We lift prayers for persons still living in the shadow of the tomb. Be with all those who mourn, who are troubled, who feel their lives lack meaning and direction. Show us how to feed the hungry, shelter the homeless, embrace the outcast, and love the lonely. We give you thanks for this community of seekers and finders that enable us to receive the good news. May the spirit of resurrection be contagious among us. Christ the Lord is Risen. He is risen in each of us. We give you thanks for filling our hearts with joy, our minds with hope, and for leading us along as an Easter people. Amen.

John 20: 1-18

Easter Sunday

O God of Love, the world around us is different today because of you. Signs of new life and new beginnings are everywhere. We rejoice and celebrate this day, for this is the day that the stones of our lives are rolled aside and the mantle of darkness is lifted. This is the day when hope dawns anew and the morning brings forth new creation. This is the day that we celebrate the resurrection of your Son.

And yet, just as the women mourned and trembled with fear on the very morning that Christ rose from the grave, there are many of your children who still live with brokenness, sadness, and tragedy, despite the presence of the Risen Christ. There are those of your children who mourn and are troubled, who feel their lives have lost meaning. Touch them today, we pray, with your transforming power that their sadness may become joy, their despair may become hope, and their defeats may become victories. For it is your transforming love that frees us from our self-made tombs and allows us to rise once again to be the persons you created us to be. It is your transforming spirit that enables us to reach out to our sisters and brothers that they might escape the crosses of poverty and injustice. It is your transforming presence that gives us meaning and purpose and new direction.

What a wondrous gift you have given us this day, O God. You have shown us once again that nothing can defeat your love for us. All of our suffering can be redeemed and transformed by the creative power of your spirit. We are your Easter people made alive by Christ's rising. The world around us is different today because of you. We praise you. Amen.

Matthew 28: 1-10; 16-20

Easter Sunday

God of resurrection, we come before you this day rejoicing in the promise of new life that this day offers to us all. Christ has risen! We feel your spirit flowing within us and among us. The cross is empty, the tomb is empty and our lives are filled with the mystery and the excitement of new life present in this day.

We pray, O God, that the spirit of resurrection might be contagious among us, that we might praise our risen Lord by renewed commitment to active discipleship. Make us new persons as you made new persons of those first disciples. Transform us from frightened, hesitant, uncommitted followers into people who face life's challenges with new meaning, new purpose, and new direction.

Enable us to make empty tombs of all our defeats. In so doing, we are empowered to see in each day, the hundreds of opportunities you make available to us to overcome doubt and despair with hope and possibility. In so doing, we are empowered to reach out to the poor and sick and confused and disheartened of the world. The world is different today because of you, O God. Christ is risen. May Christ's spirit continue to live in and through us. Amen.

John 20: 1-18

Easter Sunday

Loving God, we thank you that our fears, sorrows, and doubts are no barrier to your love for us. We thank you for the presence of the Risen Christ, a presence that comes to us in surprising ways and in unexpected places. Though we have not touched Jesus or seen him, as Thomas and the disciples, his Spirit is as present with us as it was with those early followers and as it has been with believers throughout the centuries. We pray today that each person here may be touched by the joy and empowered by your Spirit that we may be faithful witnesses to your love and grace in our hurting and fractured world.

As your Easter people, we lift our prayers to you. We lift prayers this day for all persons who are still in personal tombs, either by choice or by circumstances beyond their control. Be especially with those who mourn and bring to them the comfort and assurance that their loved one is safe in your presence. In your mercy, Lord, hear our prayers.

We lift prayers for those who are troubled, who feel their lives lack meaning and direction. Show us how to feed the hungry, shelter the homeless, embrace the outcast, and love the lonely. In your mercy, Lord, hear our prayers.

We lift prayers for all who struggle with illness, who are hospitalized, who anxiously await lab test results, who live with pain and fear of an uncertain future. Surround them with a circle of love that they may know that they are never alone. And be with all health care providers who seek to minister in your name. In your mercy, Lord, hear our prayers.

We lift prayers for families of all sizes and descriptions. Where healing of relationships needs to happen, help us to be open to opportunities for reconciliation and forgiveness. In your mercy, Lord, hear our prayers.

And finally, Loving God, we lift prayers for ourselves. You know our struggles, the places in our lives that need your healing touch. Grant us the eyes of faith and hearts of trust to see our Risen Lord in our everyday lives and to allow his Spirit to abide with us. In your mercy, Lord, hear our prayers.

We are heirs, O God, to your promise of eternal life. Let hope, therefore, prevail over despair in all circumstances. Open our hearts to the mystery of your grace all around us. Amen.   *John 20: 19-31*

Now quickly after Easter do we settle back into our everyday, normal routines, as if nothing has changed. We aren't so different from those early disciples who returned to their fishing nets. And yet things are different, and we are continually surprised and delighted by the many ways that the resurrected Christ appears in our sacred ordinary of daily living. We meet the Christ in the breaking of bread with our family, our friends, and even with strangers. We meet the Christ in our places of work; in our daily tasks and errands; in the little acts of love and support that come our way. We even meet the Christ in those unlikely places...in a hospital waiting room...in the eyes of the homeless...in the rebellious struggles of a teenager in search of identity...in the concern of a single parent for a child...in the quiet witness of our elderly.

And yet, O God, we are still reluctant to respond to that presence. It is still difficult to follow. It is still difficult to care for others the way we know we should. The Christ continually confronts us with the question, "Do you love me?" We say, "Yes, we love you," and too easily we settle back into a comfortable faith. You call us to discipleship...to feed the sheep of this world, but we continue to hold back.

Living Christ, walk among us and teach us to walk with you. Energize us, as you did those first disciples, to reach out to one another in love and in mission. Make us instruments of your peace that we might give hope to the hopeless, strength to the faltering, love to the lonely, consolation to the grieving, and faith to the faithless. Teach us to live more daringly, more expectantly, more joyfully. Transform us with your spirit that we may honor the risen Christ in active discipleship. Amen.

John 21: 15-17

Spirit of God, you choose to reveal yourself to us in so many surprising ways and in so many unexpected places. We sometimes fear that you are still dead, or maybe hiding, and we grieve and fear a future without you. As we go about our daily jobs, our old routines, our simple tasks, you are there even when we do not recognize you. And in the preparation and breaking of bread with family, friends and even strangers, you are there to strengthen us for all that lies ahead. You call us to bid us follow, and yet we still drag our feet and make excuses. We still do not know who you are or what it is you want us to do.

We profess our love for you, O Risen Christ, but we confess that our love for you is often faltering and timid. We are faithful when things are going well, when our nets and stomachs are full, but we are not so faithful in the bad times. We bury our hopes and dreams in a tomb so deep and dark, and it is our fear that seals it tight. But you return again and again to roll away the stones of fear and doubt. Forgive us for letting other things become more important than our love for you. Keep reminding us, "If you love me, feed my lambs, tend my sheep, feed my flock, follow me."

And so it is in prayer that we, as your shepherds in this world, lift our prayers and entrust to your care our very lives. We lift in our hearts this day the name of the one close to us in need of your healing, loving touch.....O Lord, hear our prayers.

We lift prayers of thanksgiving for time spent in our daily tasks and labors even as we remember those needing meaningful work and renewed confidence....O Lord, hear our prayers.

We lift up the ones you put on the road beside us, the hungry and the thirsty, the naked and the stranger, the sick and the imprisoned.....O Lord, hear our prayers.

And finally we lift prayers for this world where we are so intimately interrelated with all your children and in sacred balance with the created world. May we bless this earth by caring for it responsibly.....O Lord, hear our prayers.

In your unexpected visits, you teach us the lesson of faithful service. You enable us to regain our sight and be filled with the Holy Spirit. May we be worthy of your great love for us by responding in love to others. Amen.

Acts 9: 1-20, John 21: 1-19

Loving God, we confess that we are slow of heart to believe or accept our roles as disciples. Too often we fail to recognize and see Christ in our midst. But we are here today, gathered in this place, because we want to draw closer to the one who invites us to new life, new beginnings and new possibilities.

Enable us to be receptive to recognize Christ in the simple things. May our eyes be opened to the many ways that you choose to reveal yourself to us. May we recognize Christ in the activities of our daily living, in the smile of a child, in the touch of a friend, in the beauty of our world. May you be known to us in the breaking of our bread.

As your disciples, we are called to be your witnesses in this hurting world. Help us, O God, to live as your children, loving and serving you with all our heart and all our soul and all our might. We pray for all persons who have their own Emmaus to reach, whose eyes have not seen or recognized the presence of Christ in their midst. We pray for those who have heard the good news and now wonder what it means for their lives. We pray for those seeking to cope with the many pressures of life. We pray for those who are ill, for those who grieve, for those who face economic hardship, for those who struggle in broken relationships, and for those who face uncertain futures. Help them to realize that Christ no longer agonizes in the garden. He is no longer fixed upon the cross. He no longer lies within the tomb. Christ is risen and walks the roads we walk. We are not alone. And our ordinary is holy.

We are heirs, O God, to your promises of eternal life. Let hope, therefore, prevail over despair in all circumstances. Grant us the eyes of faith and hearts of trust to see our Risen Lord and to hear what he asks us to do. Open our hearts to the mystery and grace all around us. Amen.

Luke 24: 13-35

Loving God, how we desire to really live as your Easter people. We yearn to know you. We pray that you would enter our lives in such a way that our doubts, our fears, and our uncertainties would be transformed into confidence, trust, and an openness to your grace...and to your healing power. Enable us to be like little children, excited and empowered by the new life and new possibilities you have in store for us. In the midst of our Good Fridays, give us purpose and direction. Forgive us when we lean on our own strength instead of yours. We need to hear the word again and again—that in the midst of the dark time of our lives, you promise to be with us and to always work for what is good and true.

In this season of Easter, let us be aware of new beginnings. We lift prayers for all who suffer from physical and mental illness and give thanks for new medical breakthroughs. We lift prayers for victims of violence in our schools and among our youth. Enable us to be supporters of an education system that inspires our young people to care for one another, to value human life, and to celebrate and embrace diversity. We lift prayers for all who live in poverty and especially those who are without shelter or food. May we be shapers and workers in programs that provide food for the hungry, shelter for the homeless, and clothing for the deprived. We lift prayers for our troubled criminal justice system. Help us be involved in those places that can turn anger into resolve, despair into hope, and aimlessness into ambition. We lift prayers for our families and loved ones. Enable us to really listen to one another's concerns, hopes, and dreams, and to recognize and change those behaviors that undermine healthy relationships.

And finally, Father-Mother God, we lift prayers for ourselves. Help us to realize our worth in your sight when we are tempted to tear ourselves down for our shortcomings and failures. Help us to learn to love, respect, and take care of ourselves, modeling the love that you have first shown us. Resurrect our spirits when we are feeling down, lonely, confused, isolated, or depressed, for we are your children, precious and honored in your sight. We are your Easter people. Help us to live out that identity in all that we do and say. Amen.

Luke 24: 36b-48

oving God, sometimes we look at the world around us and wonder. We weep with those who suffer in war-torn countries. We feel such loss when we hear of the destruction to our environment and to the life it sustains. We search for your face in the eyes of the homeless, the imprisoned, the hungry, and the forgotten in our midst. We are terrified when the diagnosis we had feared becomes a reality. Yes, Lord, sometimes we look at the world around us and wonder. We call out to you. Do not leave us desolate. Do not leave us alone. Do not leave us in our fear and uncertainty.

You have promised to send your Spirit. Your Spirit comforts us when we are depressed. Your Spirit strengthens us when we are afraid. Your Spirit calms us when we are embattled. You are faithful to us even when we test you, bargain with you, abandon you, blame you. You continue to forgive us and to draw us back to yourself, for you understand the pain in our lives—the child who chooses the wrong path, the spouse who wants a divorce, the friend who drinks to mask the hurt, the one who suffers with physical limitations, the loved one who has died.

And so we pray this morning, Loving God, that you would take our sorrows and transform them into hope. With the promise of the Counselor comes an assurance that we will not be left alone. You continue to lead us as we pursue the paths of discipleship and as we seek to keep your commandments. We look to your Spirit to fill us with counsel and guidance. We look to your Spirit for strength for our journey. We look to your Spirit for an empowering love stronger than any force that should seek to defeat us.

You, O God, are our source of hope. In your presence we can wake each morning filled with a sense of wonder and we can live each day in the light of the joy that is promised. We give thanks that this church is a community of hope, living the love of Jesus for all creation and we give thanks that it is continually renewed by the fresh winds of your Spirit. Amen.

John 14: 15-21

God of all Creation, sometimes when we ponder the wonders of this world we are left in awe of its majesty. When we look upon the vastness of your oceans, the grandeur of your mountains, and the beauty of our deserts in bloom, we are aware of the holiness of all creation. We are surrounded by your glory and stunned by your splendor.

But sometimes, O God, we feel lost in the majesty of all that surrounds us. We feel lost in the crowds and in the mass of humanity. We feel that our problems and struggles are insignificant when measured against the violence, injustice, oppression, and human tragedy that we read about in the papers and see on the evening news. We even feel that our prayers may get lost, O God, at the times when we need you the most.

It is then that we need the assurance of your presence. Just as you care about the simple sparrow, the one lost sheep, and the lilies of the field, we trust you care for us. And so this morning, we offer ourselves to you as a possibility. Hold us as a tiny bud and encourage each new growth. Nurture us as fertile seeds that we might use all the potential you have given us to become a blessing to others. Grant us patience when we become impatient and frustrated, when we seem to be going nowhere, when we find ourselves stumbling along blindly.

Touch us where we are, Indwelling God. Where there is grief and sorrow, grant us your comfort. Where there is illness and hurt, grant us healing. Where there is anger and hatred, grant us peace and reconciliation. Where there is fear and despair, grant us confidence to face the future. Wherever we are, O God, give us a vision of hope and possibility. Enable us to live as Resurrection people that we might be raised to a new awareness of the wonder and sacredness of all life. Transform us from frightened, hesitant, uncommitted followers into a people given meaning, hope, purpose, and new direction through the risen Christ. Amen.

Matthew 13:31-32

God, we are witnesses to the many ways you choose to reveal yourself to us. As you appeared to the ten in Jerusalem, so too do you stand among us. And yet we do not recognize you. We are startled and frightened and we question your abiding presence in our hearts. We turn away in confusion and disbelief. We miss out on those opportunities you provide to really be in communion with you. You know our weaknesses, Divine Spirit. You know our doubts and our fears. And we pray this morning that you would open our minds to understand what it means to live with you at the center of our lives.

Give light to our minds and fill us with your power. Turn to us, that we may be healed. O Lord, hear us, we pray.

May our suffering be endured for the sake of your kingdom. Grant us patient endurance in our times of trial. O Lord, hear us, we pray.

Make your love and peace available to all those who suffer. Grant that their eyes may behold your healing grace. O Lord, hear us, we pray.

Send your Holy Spirit upon your church. Guide and uphold all who serve in your name. O Lord, hear us, we pray.

Be present to the nations and all who govern. Let them be free of evil and filled with peace. O Lord, hear us, we pray.

Look with favor on each of us. Fill us with the blessing of your healing presence. O Lord, hear us, we pray.

We have been commissioned, O Lord, as witnesses to your abundant grace and love. We have been commissioned as witnesses to share that love with others. We have been commissioned and "clothed with power from on high." By your grace may we, your humble servants, fulfill the great commission to which we have been called. In the communion of the Holy Spirit and of all the saints, we commend ourselves once again to your care through Christ our Lord. Amen.

Luke 24:35-48

Memorial Day

Loving God, too often we are content to be followers. It is easier to let someone else make the hard decisions, forge new paths or speak the words of truth that need to be spoken. But there comes a time when you call us to take up the mantle, as Elijah passed the mantle to Elisha. Those who have been followers are now called upon to lead. This morning, O God, as we come before you in prayer, we ask what mantles you would have us pick up. What tasks or situations touch our hearts and souls and nudge us from complacency to action?

We lift prayers for those who struggle with illness of mind, body and spirit...for those for whom physical or emotional pain are daily companions. We pray for those who are discouraged, depressed, or broken in spirit. Help them to know that they are not alone in their time of trial, for you are present with each of us in the dark times. In your mercy, Lord, hear our prayers.

We lift prayers for families of all description. We rejoice with those families who are celebrating the birth of a new child, grandchild, or great grandchild. We rejoice with those families who are celebrating milestones such as graduations, marriages, anniversaries, new jobs or new beginnings. Even as we share family joys, O God, we recognize that pain exists in many families. We ask your special presence with those persons struggling through divorce, addictions, domestic violence, or a breakdown in communication. Give our families strength to stand against the many forces that would tear them apart. In your mercy, Lord, hear our prayers.

We lift prayers for our country and ask that you would guide all those whom we the people have chosen to be leaders. May all who lead learn how to do justice, love mercy, and walk humbly before you. In your mercy, Lord, hear our prayers.

This Memorial Day weekend, we come to give thanks for the lives of those who have gone before us into your promised rest. You love these persons whom we name in our heart, and peace comes in knowing that they are held in your loving arms. In your mercy, Lord, hear our prayers. Amen.

II Kings 2:6-14

Ascension Sunday

Loving God, we admit that we are seldom moved by signs and visions that do not fit with our scientific world view. Our doubts are often more compelling than our faith. Yet you break through all boundaries, even the barriers we impose between heaven and earth, by continually providing glimpses of life fulfilled and eternal realities. We need to keep a vision of heaven...not as a world that runs parallel to ours, but a world that is closely interwoven with ours. We confess, O God, that in our doubt and skepticism, we limit the many ways your Spirit breaks into our lives and we limit the ways that we can encounter the eternal.

So we ask today that you would help us to hear anew the story of your bountiful love for us. May we be touched by a reality beyond our human knowing and partake of the inheritance you have promised us. Your love has been made real to us in the life of Jesus Christ and now you baptize us with the Holy Spirit and call us to be the church, Christ's body, and to serve.

And so we lift prayers, as well as commit ourselves to taking action where we can, for all who are in need. We pray for those persons facing illness, awaiting hospital test results, facing impending surgery and sometimes feeling confused and angry in trying to deal with illness as well as a medical system that, at times, overwhelms us with knowledge we do not understand. We pray for those near death and for those who have died, knowing that you are present with them and their loved ones even as they walk through the valley of the shadow of death. We pray, O God, for ourselves and for those we care about that we might seek out ways to lessen the stress and anxiety in our lives so we can rejoice in the beauty of your creation and celebrate the goodness of the many ways you choose to reveal yourself in our everyday lives. You continue to empower our lives through your grace and the constancy of your love for each of us. May we go out into the world open to the signs of your presence. Amen.

Acts 1:1-11

Ascension Sunday

O God, as we come before you today, we are so grateful for the very real presence of your Son even as we celebrate the triumph of his ascension. You have not left us comfortless. You have clothed us with "power from on high." You have given us strength. You have exalted us and lifted us above our earthly trials even as you have drawn your Son to live and reign with you. We are the grateful recipients of a commission...of a promise...and of a blessing.

As recipients of your commission, promises and blessing, we ask that we might feel your special presence as we return to our personal Jerusalems. We ask that we might be empowered and strengthened for the tasks that lie ahead. We ask that those who feel lonely, those who are grieving, those who have given up, those who face difficult decisions, and those who struggle with illness, might be touched today by your presence and be comforted by your promise to always be with us.

Just as your Son drew all to himself by faith, enable us to be witnesses to the promise of new life you offer us through repentance. Enable us to be witnesses to the freedom to begin again that comes with the forgiveness of sins. Enable us to be witnesses to life eternal even as we live and serve you in our lives today.

All these things we pray in the name of Jesus Christ our Lord, who lives and reigns with you, in the unity of the Holy Spirit, one God, now and forever. Amen.

Luke 24:44-53

Pentecost

Divine Spirit, today especially we give thanks for the gift of peace you have bestowed upon us, your disciples, by the Holy Spirit. Just as the Spirit moved Christ's disciples throughout the centuries, so may we catch that Spirit moving among us, rekindling our faith, and transforming all that is hard and dead into new life and new commitment in Christ.

We seek your forgiveness this day for all the walls of hostility we have built which separate us from one another. We seek your forgiveness for our failure to share our gifts and talents with others. We seek forgiveness for the lack of care we have shown towards the created world. Even as we seek forgiveness, we are empowered to move ahead in confidence and hope because of the assurance that we have already been forgiven and accepted by you.

And so, O God, today we celebrate your Spirit which unites your people everywhere, people of every color and of every nation. We celebrate the peace of Christ that ties us together, enabling us to be agents of reconciliation in this church and in the world. We celebrate the Spirit that moves us to nurture one another, to challenge one another, to celebrate with one another. We celebrate with the young people of this church who have been touched by the winds of your Spirit and who this day witness to their faith through baptism and confirmation. May the mighty wind of your Spirit lift all of us to higher visions, to greater dreams and to a renewed strength to make those visions and dreams a reality in this world. May we be opened today to the new creation you seek to bring about within and among us, through Jesus Christ our Lord. Amen.

John 20: 19-22

Pentecost/Confirmation Sunday

Loving God, we give thanks for the gift of the Holy Spirit which you have sent to us, drawing us into the body of Christ and making holy the commonplace. The fresh winds of your spirit are like a cool, refreshing breeze that flows over our hungry souls. You bestow upon us a variety of gifts that we might carry on the work of Christ in this hurting world. We confess, O God, that often we have difficulty even recognizing and acknowledging our gifts. We confess that sometimes we misuse the gifts you grant us. And we confess that at times we are reluctant to use our gifts to build up the body of Christ, thinking others will carry on your work in our place.

And so, this morning, we recommit ourselves to be Christ's body in the world. We recommit ourselves to seek healing in relationships, mind, body, and spirit. We recommit ourselves to speak the words of justice and compassion. We recommit ourselves to work for unity and reconciliations in difficult situations. We lift up and remember those who have gone before us, who have fought the good fight, who have finished the race and who now celebrate life eternal. And we recommit ourselves to move forward in their memory, to make the vision of your kingdom a reality for all of your children.

And on this day of Pentecost, as we celebrate the birth of the church, we pray that you would come to us and empower us with your Spirit that unites your people everywhere, people of every color and of every nation. May we be open today to the new creation you seek to bring about within and among us, through Jesus Christ our Lord. Amen.

1 Cor. 12:4-13

82

God, the fresh winds of your Spirit are like a cool, refreshing breeze that flows over our hungry souls. You breathe on us the breath of life, and we are empowered to experience new life. But we have to admit, Loving God, that sometimes we are left wondering when we experience the mystery of your presence with us. Like Nicodemus, we seek your answers, but we are more comfortable when your response conforms to our logical and rational thinking.

You tell us that unless we are born anew, we cannot see the Kingdom of God. Help us to understand that we are constantly given opportunities to begin anew. Teach us again how to see, but this time through your eyes. Teach us again to walk, this time in your shoes. Teach us again to feel, this time through your senses. Teach us again to love, this time with your heart.

Help us to be born from above and inspire us with the confidence that you will be with us in our life journey. Help us to let go of those things that hold us down. Comfort those among us who struggle with illness, who are overcome by loss, who are held prisoner by addictions, who are despondent over their present life situation. You, Loving God, come to offer hope, to change the circumstances of our lives and to offer us the promise of eternal life. For we are a people born of water and of the Spirit and sent out as witnesses to a hurting world. Amen.

John 3:1-17

We come before you this morning, O God, in a spirit of thanksgiving and celebration. We are thankful that all who live in faith are able to become your children and heirs of your promises and covenant with us. We celebrate the children we baptize this morning, for they are putting on Christ and entering into a new world where we are all one in Jesus Christ. We long for the day when all human distinctions are ended, when ethnic, gender, and social distinctions are removed. We wish to live, as our baptism vows declare, as ones who put our whole trust in your grace to live "in union with the church which Christ has opened to people of all ages, nations and races."

We confess, Divine Spirit, that we have not lived up to the vision you have set before us. We have not coped well with the confusion and complexity of the many problems facing the cities and nations of this world. We seek your help in becoming more sensitive to the needs of those living with poverty and injustice. May this sensitivity to the needs of others begin with us, with our close relationships and with our families. Heal our relationships in need of your grace. Encourage us to be caring fathers, loving mothers, and compassionate friends. Help us to live up to the grand inheritance you have graciously bestowed upon us according to your promise.

Loving God, send your Spirit upon us and fill us with your love and grace. Help us become one family in Christ as we seek to live out a future of possibility and hope. Amen.

Galatians 3:23-29

oly God, we confess that the winds of Spirit have not moved us much lately. Too often the busyness of our lives saps our energy and blinds us to the wind and fire of your presence. Too often we are quick to judge the actions of those around us. Too often we are so hard on ourselves for personal failures and misguided allegiances, that we leave little room for your grace and love.

More and more we discover, Spirit God, that contradictions and paradox surround our lives. Like the good seeds and the weeds, we find the good and evil sharing the same fertile soil. We find ourselves abiding in the light and the shadows even as we ponder the mystery of what it means to lose life in order to gain life. We live the paradox of feeling empty sadness over a loved one no longer with us, while, at the same time, our hearts are filled with thanksgiving for wonderful memories that no one can take from us.

Teach us, Divine Spirit, to live the contradictions of our lives. In the midst of our noisy, active days, enable us to hear silence and appreciate solitude. Enable us to grow in faith and trust in our personal lives that your Spirit will move us from solitude to action in community. Help us to understand our weaknesses that we might also recognize and use our strengths to live peaceably with others and to overcome evil with good.

In our journey, may we discover the joy of obedience that frees us to rejoice in hope. In our journey, we discover that your Spirit whispers through life's tensions and contradictions, moving us from broken people to a fullness and wholeness of life in Christ. May all our struggles and pain be transformed through the cross into a joyful response to the many ways you reveal yourself in our lives. We give you thanks, O God, for your patient and persistent love for us. Amen.

Matthew 13:24-30   Romans 12:9-21

oving Creator, you continue to surprise us and catch us off guard. Just when we think we have figured out who you are and what you want, you come to us in surprising ways, revealing secrets that have been hidden. You catch us unaware. Sometimes we even miss out on an encounter with you because we do not recognize your presence in our midst.

So, O God of Mystery, we pray that you would keep us open and attentive to the gift of your Spirit. May we, like Abraham, recognize you in the face of strangers. May we welcome each person we meet with care and kindness, for we never know when we may be welcoming you. Grant that we may not turn you away, unaware of the many diverse ways you choose to reveal yourself to us.

We, like the apostles, are called to go out into the vineyards of the world, to labor in your fields, and to work for the long-anticipated coming of your Kingdom. We are called to listen and to respond to the beckonings of your Spirit. We are called to open ourselves to your healing that we might, in turn, offer ourselves in service to others. We, as ordinary people, are called to tap abilities and gifts we never knew we had and to use those gifts in a hurting world. We identify with those who are sick, those who are outcasts, those who are confused, and we hold them in our hearts and prayers. In praying so, may you release in us healing possibilities we never knew existed and may we be fruitful laborers in the vineyards of this world. Amen.

Genesis 18:1-15   Matthew 9:35-10:8

Sometimes, O God, the things you ask us to do or to endure seem impossible. You make demands of us that test us, and yet, that very testing helps to shape our faith. You push and prod us. You nudge us. You urge us to take actions that move us toward growth and completeness. Even when we would rather turn away, you hold us with a love that does not let us go.

We give you thanks, Loving God, for the vision that those of faith have set before us. Like Abraham, we learn that you continually offer new life, new possibilities and new beginnings to those who trust in your saving grace. We commit ourselves once again to taking the risks of discipleship, knowing that you will raise us up and equip us for our tasks. We rejoice in your promise to be with us always and to never abandon us in our times of need. Many of us come to you this morning with those needs heavy on our hearts. And so in confidence and trust, we lift our concerns to you.

We lift prayers for our world and for the victims of oppression and injustice. Help us to move from complacency to compassionate action in serving the hungry, the homeless and the poor in our midst. Hear our prayers, O God.

We lift prayers for the unity of all your children. Empower us to remove those obstacles that divide us by gender, social status, economic class, skin color and language. Hear our prayers, O God.

We lift prayers for those who face an uncertain future due to economic conditions, difficult transitions, or struggling relationships. Hear our prayers, O God.

We lift prayers for those among us who are sick and seek your healing presence in their lives. Comfort those in sorrow and those who grieve the loss of a loved one. Hear our prayers, O God.

We lift prayers for ourselves, that we might grow in our faith and trust so that we can take the creative risks necessary to bring wholeness and healing to all people and to ourselves. Hear our prayers, O God.

For your abounding grace, unlimited love, and infinite mercy sustain us through all our days. When we turn away in anger or fear, you are there to persistently call us from within. When we seek you in distress, you find us and provide for all our needs. You do not test us beyond our strengths, but rather you provide the way that we might endure whatever comes our way. We give you thanks for your steadfast love for us. Amen. *Genesis 22:1-14*

There are times in our lives, O God, when you open the gates of heaven and we catch a glimpse of the way you would have things be. We catch sight of the path of righteousness and peace that you would have us follow. You call us, as you called Jacob, despite all our flaws and weaknesses, to enter into a new relationship with you.

We thank you, Divine Spirit, that as we face that which lies ahead, we do so with the assurance that we have been the recipients of your abundant grace and the free gift of righteousness. We give thanks for your guiding Spirit that has been present throughout history and sustains us in our journeys this day. We give thanks for your Son, Jesus, who shows us the way to life abundant.

We ask your special blessing and presence this day with our youth and other persons who are graduating and who are setting out on new paths. We celebrate and give you thanks for the beginning of summer, for the opportunities for rest, relaxation and renewal. In our dreams and times of rest, you fill us with the promise and hope for the future. In our waking hours, you call us to the task of opening the gateway of heaven to those of your children who are hurting and in need.

For your promise to continually be with us, we give you thanks. Help us discover those holy and sacred places in our lives. Set before us a vision of your heaven. Strengthen us to listen to your call and to work with you in all we do. Amen.

Genesis 28:10-17

Loving God, each day you make of us a new creation. Through the Holy Spirit, you have planted your words of wisdom, your promise of hope and the assurance that we can wipe the dust from our feet, and begin anew. You have given us the harvest of your redeeming grace, that no matter what our shortcomings and failures, you have sent your Spirit to guide us and enlighten our path. When we are weak or discouraged, you give us faith, courage, and patience to keep on going. And so we lift our prayers to you knowing that you already hear the unspoken prayers of our hearts.

We pray for our cities and for the turmoil we see on the daily news. Give us courage to confront the causes of hatred and fear wherever they may occur. In your mercy, Lord, hear our prayers.

We pray for our homes and families. We give thanks for the love and joy that families share. But we also recognize those relationships that are strained or broken. We lift those relationships to you and pray for the grace to seed reconciliation. In your mercy, Lord, hear our prayers.

We lift prayers for all who are single, by choice, because of divorce, or because of the loss of a beloved spouse. Help us to remember that "alone" does not have to mean lonely. In your mercy, Lord, hear our prayers.

We pray for those who face illness and hospitalization. We pray for those undergoing medical treatments with an uncertain outcome. Grant them and their loved ones the peace and assurance of your presence in all the difficult times of life. In your mercy, Lord, hear our prayers.

O God, forgive us when we, as your laborers in the field, have sowed crops of bigotry, intolerance, selfishness, and indifference. May we be moved to live by the Spirit so that the fruit of our harvest will be love and compassion toward all. In your mercy, Lord, hear our prayers.

You, Loving God, send us out as laborers for the harvest. May we hear your call and respond where we are needed. May we go into the world to proclaim the good news of your grace which leads to a peace which passes all understanding. Amen.

Galatians 6:7-16   *Luke 10:1-12*

reator God, we come to you today with all our questions about the meaning of life. We read newspaper headlines about war, hatred and violence here at home and with our sisters and brothers in other lands. We experience our own disappointments and frustrations and regrets. We hurt for those we care about when they go through difficult times.

And all the time, O God, we wonder. We come to church and, in these times of quiet, we are moved to really look at our lives. And we wonder. We wonder at your presence that calms our fears...that stills our hearts...that gives meaning in the midst of all the contradictions we experience.

We wonder too at the turbulence and agitation you cause within us. You stir us from complacency to involvement in hurt we see around us. You call us to be a bit like Jesus...to really do something...to make our lives count for something...to be a friend, lover, helper, and healer to others. In reaching out so, we are often surprised by your presence that gives us the meaning for our lives that we often seek. And again we wonder.

Today we lay before you all those contradictory feelings. We cry and we laugh with you. We feel contentment and peace. We rage out at injustice. We reach out in confidence. We pull back, seeking healing within. We feel fulfilled, renewed, and whole. We feel uninvolved, self-absorbed and powerless.

Help us, O God, to admit and accept all these feelings. Keep alive our sense of wonder that in the midst of the mystery of life, your Spirit continually moves among us...seeking us out...renewing our faith in the essential goodness of life...empowering us to work for the best we can imagine despite the worst that we experience. Amen.

oving God, how easily we relate to those disciples filled with fear and trembling, as their small boat is swamped in the darkness of the night. Like the unpredictable waves of the sea, our lives are rarely placid and calm. Rather we are rocked by change and circumstance, often beyond our control. And when our very foundations are shaken, we often can't see past our present fear. In the midst of life's storms, we find it hard to really trust. It is not easy to sense your presence or to feel inner peace when life events toss us to and fro. Sometimes when we need you the most, you seem asleep and deaf to our cries for help. We forget that we share the same boat and that you will not abandon us to the storm.

And so we ask your forgiveness, O God, for our lack of trust, for our need to be in control, for our misplaced anger, for looking the other way when we face issues of justice or inequity, for living more for ourselves than for others. We ask your special presence this day, Gentle Spirit, to touch those who live in fear— fear of unemployment, fear associated with health issues, fear of domestic violence, fear of growing old, fear of letting go of old habits and addictions, fear of change, fear of those who are different from us, fear of rejection, and the fear that comes when we feel helpless and abandoned by you. Help us to turn to you for assurance and guidance. Only you can provide a safe haven in our times of distress. Only you can command the wind and the sea to be still and give us the inner peace we need so much. Christ of all ages, strengthen our trust in you, in each other, and in ourselves. Amen.

Mark 4:35-41

Loving God, we confess that often life is not easy. Like the Apostle Paul, we all have our own thorns, whether they be thorns of the flesh or of the spirit. Like Paul, we have a choice of how we understand the hardships and trials that come our way. If we place our trust in human strength alone, we find ourselves in a position of weakness. Help us, O God, to not be bitter, resentful, or angry when we are faced with adversity. Help us to see that our weaknesses can indeed become our strengths and that your grace is sufficient for all our needs. Grant us that humility to yield to you our will, that you might adapt it to your purpose.

Wherever we are, you are with us. We celebrate and give thanks for your presence with us in all that we do. We are your covenant people and you are our God.

We lift prayers for all who struggle with thorns of the flesh or spirit, that your strength might be sufficient for all needs.

The prayers spoken, and the prayers you know that are in our hearts we lift to you in the assurance that you receive our prayers and that you receive us just as we are. Continue to guide us toward authentic, present, and meaningful service. Amen.

2 Cor. 12: 2-10

We give you thanks, Divine Spirit, that we have been liberated in Christ. Yet, we confess, O God, that freedom is often more difficult for us than slavery. It is hard to shake some of the habits of servitude. And it is difficult to accept the new responsibilities and choices that freedom opens to us. Like the Israelites, after the exodus, who found themselves longing for their former life of servitude, we too find our freedom in Christ difficult and demanding.

You call us to exercise our freedom in the context of the community. You call us to bear one another's burdens. You call us to forgiveness and reconciliation. You call us to love our neighbors as ourselves. Even as you call us to freedom in Christ, you also empower us with your love and your grace.

As we celebrate Independece Day, we lift our prayers for the founders of our country. May we have the grace to maintain our liberties in righteousness and peace for all your people. In your mercy, Lord, hear our prayers.

We lift our prayaers for our earth, that all of us might treat your creation with reverence and care. In your mercy, Lord, hear our prayers.

We pray for comfort and healing for those among us who suffer in mind, body and spirit. Give us courage and hope in our troubles and a vision of hope for the future. In your mercy, Lord, hear our prayers.

And we lift prayers for ourselves, for the forgiveness of all our shortcomings, known and unknown, for those things we have done and those we have left undone, for closing you out at the times we need you most. Enable us to begin again to serve you in newness of life. In your mercy, Lord, hear our prayers.

And so, once again we let go of our fear and anxiety and put our trust in you. Once again we are refreshed, renewed, restored, reconciled. Once again we are empowered to face the changes and uncertainty in our lives. Once again you awaken us with your grace and we regain a sense of wonder. Once again we celebarte our freedom as a country and our freedom in Christ. Amen.

Galatians 5:1, 13-15

God, we come this morning seeking to be in relationship with you...seeking answers to those questions and prayers spoken in our hearts. It would be so much easier, God, if you would make your will known to us through spectacular signs and grand interventions. We like things visible and spelled out. We look for the dramatic; the burning bushes, the floods, the lightning bolts.

Instead we find our lives unmarked by any cosmic signs of your presence. So often you seem hidden and silent to us. Like the prophet Elijah, we are tempted to run away...to hide from your presence...to nurse our wounds and regrets.

While looking for the dramatic signs, Gentle God, we often overlook the quiet, subtle evidences of your presence. In looking for the dramatic, we so often miss the small miracles...the touch of a child, a loved one's understanding glance, a friend's act of kindness. In looking for the dramatic, we often miss your still, small voice that seeks us out in our hiding places and fills us with your grace. Only then are we empowered to step out in faith once again...to become instruments of your healing and assuring presence to those who are weakened by disease, those who are troubled and discouraged by life's cares and concerns, and those who are suffering from losses in their life.

When we want immediate answers, precise directions, and open doors, O God, help us to be patient with small steps, quiet nudges, and everyday miracles. Teach us, O God, to listen with our hearts. All we really need to hear is your whisper. Amen.

1 Kings 19: 1-15

Divine Spirit, how we want to be healed. You know our hurts and our pain. You know the longings of our hearts. You know those places in mind, spirit, and body that are in need of your healing touch. Sometimes we are reluctant to reach out to you with our whole heart. We want to be healed, but our lack of trust and faith prevents us from reaching out to you.

Help us, O God, to have the faith of the unnamed woman with a hemorrhage. Help us to reach out for your helping, healing, life-giving presence. Give us the courage to step through the crowds and other obstacles that would prevent us from being close to you. Enable us to be free of all that would limit us or hold us back from becoming the persons you would have us be.

Yes, Loving God, we come before you as your children, yearning to be made whole. We pray for all who are in need of healing. We pray that you might hear the yearnings of our hearts and answer us. In the quiet of this time, O God, we listen expectantly for your whispers of grace. We open our lives to you now to receive your blessings. Receive us in our pain and brokenness and let us be healed. Restore to us a vision of your world where each person lives and walks in the light of your love. In the name of the Risen Christ, we pray. Amen.

Mark 5: 24b-34

ometimes, O God, we seek your presence in prayer, but the words just don't come easily. We want to be open to your Spirit, but the knowledge of our own weakness makes us close down and pull back from your love and from the love of those around us. When we feel frightened, alone, confused, and frustrated with our own feeble efforts, it is your Spirit that intercedes with sighs too deep for words. We can let go in trust and faith that you know our needs and desires even before we are able to put them into words. We can rest in your presence knowing that you are involved in our daily lives, working to bring forth that which is good and true.

We rededicate ourselves this morning to your purposes, Divine Spirit. Knowing in faith that you are working for the good in all circumstances, we lift our concerns and prayers to you. We lift prayers for our world and its leaders that justice, peace, and righteousness might prevail over those forces that would degrade or dehumanize your people. We ask your special presence be with those who suffer loss because of floods and other natural disasters. May they see your face in the compassionate stranger who reaches out with a helping hand. Be with those who face illness, both physical and mental, that they might be restored, refreshed, and renewed by your grace. Bring comfort to those who grieve, hope to those who are without hope, and assurance to those who struggle with direction in life.

Humble us, Loving God, that we might be receptive to the gift of your unfailing grace. Forgive us when we act as if we have all the answers. Forgive us for the times we manipulate or use others. Forgive us when we exploit situations for our own benefit. Forgive us when we pursue our own personal needs at the expense of others.

We thank you for the abundant love and grace you make available to us in spite of our weaknesses and shortcomings. We thank you for the gift of your Son and for the assurance that nothing can separate us from your love. Your Spirit reaches out to us in our weakness with strength and power beyond our understanding. Amen.

Romans 8:26-39

hank you, O God, for the many ways you show your love for us. You heal us when we are wounded. You protect us when we are vulnerable. You come to us when we are alone.

Yet we, like the centurion, are sometimes reluctant to come to you and to receive you into our hearts and homes. The awareness of our shortcomings is ever before us. So often we feel unworthy of the extravagant love you shower upon us. Forgive us, O God, for reducing your world to the size of our prejudices. Forgive us for limiting Christ to conform to our narrow expectations. Give us the faith of the centurion that we might be healed and made whole. Give us the compassion of the centurion that we might take risks to bring healing and wholeness to others. Give us the insight of the centurion to know that the power to heal belongs to you alone and is available to all peoples regardless of wealth, stature, or worth. It is in your love that we place our trust and our hope as we lift our prayers of petition.

We lift up those persons in need of your healing touch today and most especially the person we now name in our hearts. O Lord, hear our prayers.

We lift our prayers for little children, for our youth, for single people, for the elderly that they might be surrounded by your love and be assured of their potential and worth. O Lord, hear our prayers.

We pray that your healing power might flow into our hurting world, that politicians might govern with compassion and that world leaders might work for the welfare of the least of their people. O Lord, hear our prayers.

We bring before you prayers for ourselves...for our own hurts, our loneliness, our grief, our fears, our broken relationships, and our anxiety about the future. O Lord, hear our prayers.

We pray that each of us might live a life of faith and trust. Fill us with the blessing of wholeness of mind, spirit, and body. O Lord, hear our prayers.

All these things we can pray with confidence, for, as your children, we are chosen and called by name. And so we lift our prayers, both spoken and the prayers of our hearts, Divine Spirit, that in your infinite grace, you might bring us home to you...and to ourselves. Amen.

Luke 7:1-10

ver-present and ever-loving God, our prayers to you are but a response to your abundant love for us. When we are anxious, you are there to calm our fears. When we are grieving, you are there to surround us with your gentle presence. When we have hurt others or hurt ourselves, you are there to say, "My child, begin again." When we face difficult choices in our lives, you are there to guide, uphold, and strengthen us.

And so, Gracious God, we place before you our fragmented, harried and confusing lives that you might help us catch glimpses of beauty and joy. We place before you the people we know who hurt; the struggling child, the frustrated parent, the fragile relationship, the crisis of health; that you might teach us the sacrament of care as we reach out to others. We place before you our world, and those persons yearning for justice, freedom and peace.

Move us, Spirit God, beyond our immediate wants, needs, and expectations to the new life you offer to us. Your gifts to us reach far beyond our limited imagination. You have nourished us with your love. Enable us now to share the loaves and fishes of our lives with our sisters and brothers who are in need of a symbol of compassion and hope. We give you thanks, Redeeming God, for your abundant gift of love that, like the loaves and fishes, is never exhausted. You provide us with the love of Christ which surpasses all knowledge. You empower us to move from our fears to a life of trust and faith. Amen.

John 6:1-15

oving God, we give you thanks for your countless blessings in our lives. Whatever our needs may be this morning, you are here to surround us with your compassion and care. You are approachable and seek to be in relationship with us.

But often, O God, we fail to do our part. We get busy and distracted and don't take the time to nurture the intimate relationship we yearn to have with you. Sometimes we are afraid to come before you because we feel unworthy. Other times, we know we are in need, but we are unable to put the deep yearnings of our hearts into words. At these times, we need to be reminded that you already know our needs and desires, and you accept and love us just as we are. All that you ask us to do is to reach out - to ask, to seek and to knock. Like a friend at midnight, you have promised to rise and answer us when we call.

And so, this morning, we come before you boldly asking for what we need this day to be the whole persons you created us to be. In silence, we lift before you our own name or the name of another as we seek your healing touch.

We lift to you the name of one who is struggling with illness of mind, body, or spirit.

We lift to you the name of one who grieves the loss of a loved one.

We lift to you the name of one in need of forgiveness or who needs to forgive, who needs to listen and understand, in a relationship that is strained.

We lift to you the name of one who feels alone and hopeless because of unemployment, financial worries, stress, or lack of meaningful direction of life.

When we come asking, Loving God, continue to receive us. When we seek guidance, help us to be directed by your Spirit. When we knock at the door, help us to hear you call us by name and invite us to enter into your presence. Amen.

Luke 11:1-13

Loving God, we thank you this day for the gift of your son Jesus who brought good news to the oppressed and liberation to all of us who are held in some sort of bondage. We come before you in gratitude, giving thanks that we are made in your image, called according to your purpose, and commissioned to do your will. Help us to discover gifts we never knew we had and enable us to use them in behalf of all your children. Yes, we are of one spirit and brought together through baptism into one body, your church.

The church is called to be one body with different parts to make it function. And yet we often sever that one body through division, suspicion, fear, and hostility. In doing so we take from one another what belongs to us all. Forgive us, O God, and by your grace, make us one again in Christ. Enable us to come together this day to explore the meaning of our membership in the body of Christ.

O God of Change, Invitation, and Challenge, let us hear your words to us this day. Divert our attention from those things that divide and misdirect our commitment. Release us, that we may receive your spirit. Transform us, and we shall know a world transformed. Amen.

1 Cor. 12:1-13

Luke 4:14-21

O God of judgment and liberation, sometimes we don't understand our own actions. We think of ourselves as religious persons and yet we know that our thoughts and actions are not always as they ought to be. We acknowledge the existence of evil...of temptation...of sin. Our best intentions often become distorted. It is a struggle, O God, to be the persons you would have us be.

And yet, in all our weakness, you offer us hope. In all our despair, you offer us your grace, and love that sets us free and enables us to begin again.

We give you thanks for delivering us from our ways that bind us and imprison us. You sent Moses to deliver your children from bondage in Egypt. You sent Jesus Christ to liberate us from the evil forces that tempt and threaten us. And you send each one of us to be your instrument of salvation in this world today.

We are called, as a loved and reconciled people, to reach out where there is pain, brokenness, and injustice. Restore to us the vision of a world where the poor are loved, where the outcasts are given a home, where the sick receive healing, purpose, and meaning in their lives. Restore to us the vision of your church in mission.

Grant us wisdom and surround us with guidance, O God, as we seek to act out Christ's call. It is in Jesus Christ that we find true freedom and the joy to live according to the Spirit. It is in Christ that we experience your mercy, your compassion, and your love. Amen.

Romans 7:14-25

Waiting is so hard for us, Lord. We would rather be involved in all kinds of tasks that distract us from the waiting. Restless activity and the trivialities of life keep our attention. But just as the servant was rewarded by his master for his patient waiting for the master's return, so, too, will we be rewarded in a very personal way. We need your help, O God, to be that kind of servant. We find it difficult to just watch and wait in anticipation of your coming to us.

We yearn for you so. We strain our ears to hear your knock upon the door of our hearts. Help us to wait in openness and receptivity. Help us to not be distracted by the things of this world that pull us away from our waiting on your coming.

This kind of waiting in patience is even harder when you seem to be absent from us. But we watch and listen. And like the returning master, you come to us. You always reward our patient waiting, our receptivity, our alertness, by inviting us to sit down and eat and be served by you. For you, Loving God, are the bread of life and the living water that we so desire.

In the midst of our waiting, we lift our prayers to you. We pray for all persons, including ourselves, who hurt, who are lonely, who grieve, who are afraid, who struggle with broken relationships, or who are anxious about the future. Still our fears with your healing touch, for you come to us in the most unexpected and surprising ways. For this we give you thanks and praise your name. Amen.

Luke 12:35-40

All-loving God, we come together from many different places and bring with us our individual experiences, problems and needs. Some of us come with self-doubt and fear of facing the many trials in our lives. Others come with false pride, thinking that we alone possess all the resources to make things turn out right.

Yet each of us has been called into covenant with you, and called to be accountable to that covenant. You tell us we need "to do justice," thus caring for and protecting equity in all human relationships. You tell us "to love kindness" and to be with those in need or in trouble. You tell us "to walk humbly" with you and to submit our wills to your will. It sounds so simple, O God, and yet, we confess our failure to be faithful. We go our own way, forgetting your many blessings and saving acts on our behalf. We are proud and boast of our own virtue instead of relying on your grace.

And all the time we yearn still to restore our relationship with you. We seek your healing presence. We need to be made whole. For it is in Jesus Christ that you have shown us the extent of your love for us. It is the example of His love that has shown us how to do justly, to love kindness, and to walk humbly with you.

In faith we lift our prayers to you. We pray for all who suffer persecution and oppression in this world. We pray for all who grieve, who have suffered loss, who feel alone in facing an uncertain future. We pray for all who are sick, who are in hospitals, who wait the results of hospital tests with apprehension. We pray for those whose family relationships have broken down, for those going through divorce or separation and for those who struggle for understanding and love. We pray for ourselves that, surrounded by so great a cloud of witnesses, we might lay aside every weight and sin which binds us. We pray that we might run with perseverance, endurance and joy, the race you have set before us. All these prayers we lay humbly before you as offerings of ourselves and our very lives. Amen.

Micah 6:1-8   Hebrews 12:1-2,12-17

entle Spirit, there are so many times when, like the disciples, we are in a boat that comes upon stormy water. There are so many times when our fears grip us and we look desperately for a way to still the storm, to calm the fears. We are so busy trying to control the situation that we fail to recognize your presence with us in the boat. Our lack of trust and faith is evident in our frenzied need to take control, to try to calm the storms within and without.

But you are present with us if only we would just "be" instead of trying to "do." You come quietly to us in the still places of mystery. You meet us where we are, in the midst of our ordinary lives. Help us, O God, to be truly open to your presence. Help us to experience for ourselves your love and care and grace. Help us to know that there is peace on the other side of our storms. Enable us to have faith enough to face our frustrations, our grief, our pain, our confusion, our loneliness, and to receive from you the simple gift of your abiding presence. For all of life is touched by you. Enable us to see our storms through your eyes. Enable us to let go of our expectations, of our preconceived ideas of what should happen, and allow you to surprise us and fill us with wonder and awe. Enable us to recognize you in mystery...and be graced by your presence. Amen.

Mark 4:35-41

Gracious God, we cannot hide from you. You know the secrets of our hearts, our aspirations and our lack of confidence, our willingness to accept challenge and change, and our times of resistance and reluctance to follow your leadings. And yet you love us still. You are always with us to guide, protect, and nurture us along our path. You hold us in arms of grace, uplift us on wings of hope, and care for us in surprising ways. For this we lift our praise and gratitude.

Yet there are times when we act as if we were still living in the dominion of darkness. We have passed by our neighbors and ignored opportunities to extend mercy. We have made excuses and then acted in our own self-interest when confronted with issues of injustice, oppression, and greed. O God, if our future is to be better, help us become one family in your name. Enable us to love and show compassion toward the sick, the homeless, the jobless, the victims of natural disasters, and the ones who have lost hope in our midst. Help us to do our best to love and serve where we live, work, and play.

Because we are the recipients of your care in Christ, we have been entrusted with the care of others and of all the created world. You are there to help us through the transitions in our lives. You offer us the strength and grace to face the regrets of our past and to move forward into the present, accepting the mantle of responsibility that has been passed to us by those who have gone before. May we be worthy of your trust so that we can love others as you have loved us. May we be faithful in all our tasks. And may you touch our lives, every once in a while, with a miracle. Amen.

2 Kings 2:1, 6-14

Col. 1:1-14

ometimes, O God, we don't feel like we are the salt of the earth. We don't shine as a light to the world. We don't give you the glory that is due. We get caught up in our own needs, desires, and activities. We like to think that we are in control and so we act as if we are. And yet in doing so, we are breaking our covenant with you. In forgetting that we are the salt of the earth, we are abandoning the covenant made between you and your people.

So we come this morning, seeking restoration. We come seeking wholeness. We come to let go of our own desires and be only what you would have us become. Have mercy on each of us as we seek to renew our covenant with you once again. In the confidence that you hear us, we lift our prayers to you.

We remember the poor, and ask that we may find ways to feed them; and the sick, that they may receive healing. In your mercy, Lord, hear our prayers.

We pray for the grieving, that their hearts may be comforted; for the lonely, that they might find relationship, and for the fearful, that they may be given confidence. In your mercy, Lord, hear our prayers.

We lift prayers for the doubtful, that they may have faith; for the cynical, that they may experience trust; and for all children and young people, that they may be kept from harmful ways. In your mercy, Lord, hear our prayers.

We pray for our church that it might be given courage, strength, and endurance. In your mercy, Lord, hear our prayers.

And we pray for ourselves that we might find you in quietness and follow you in faithfulness all the days of our lives. In your mercy, Lord, hear our prayers.

Deepen our compassion, O God. Stir up our commitment. Help us to live each day throughout the year as children of the covenant, created, called out, and commissioned by him whose name is above every name, even Jesus our Lord. Amen.

Leviticus 2:11-16   Matthew 5:13-16

entle Spirit, you call us to love one another, as Christ has loved us. You call us to sacrifice for one another, as Christ has sacrificed for us. You call us to forgive one another, as Christ has forgiven us. How we want to follow your will for our lives. But the reality is that our anger, bitterness, resentments, frustrations, and judgments of others get in the way. Our human emotions too often control our actions, and we end up doing or saying those things that break down community and understanding, rather than building up the body of Christ.

And so, as we ask for your forgiveness, we also ask for your strength and guidance as we seek once again to be the people you would have us to be. We need your forgiveness for we are hard enough on ourselves. We feel the weight of our guilt and shame and easily condemn ourselves. We stand in need of your grace to free us from the burdens we carry, to equip us to be your beloved children and to live in love and peace with one another.

As members of the body of Christ, we lift prayers for our community and for ourselves. For our nation, we lift prayers for relief from the increased violence and fear that are so prevalent in our cities. We pray for the homeless, the unemployed, the addicted, those suffering form physical or mental illnesses, and those who grieve some loss in their lives. We lift prayers for our elderly that they might live with dignity and respect. We lift prayers for our youth that they might be filled with visions of hope for the future. We lift prayers for each of us that we might find purpose and meaning in our lives.

Lead us, Loving God, so we may imitate your ways and walk in your love. All of this we ask in the name of the one who said, "I am the bread of life. Whoever comes to me will never be hungry, and whoever believes in me will never be thirsty." It is in Christ's name that we pray. Amen.

Ephesians 4:25-5:2

oving God, your mercy and compassion for us are revealed in so many ways. Too often we like to think we are in control and can handle things ourselves. It is hard for us to ask for help or to depend on others. Sometimes it is even hard for us to really trust in your saving grace. We get caught up in our individualism, in our desire for independence and self-sufficiency, and we forget how intimately interconnected and interrelated we really are.

And yet you continue to watch over us, like you watched over Moses among the bulrushes. You send caring and compassionate people our way when we are most in need. You guide us through the swift currents of life and bring us to a place of safety...to a place called home. You work in surprising ways to make our journeys possible. We expect that you will send the strong, the powerful, and the wise. Instead you choose the weak, the simple, and the downtrodden. You use fragile vessels such as ourselves to bring love, kindness, and justice.

And so, this morning, we ask that you would use us in whatever ways you choose. Where there is suffering, discouragement, and despair, help us to respond with compassion. Where there is illness, grief, and estrangement, help us to respond with loving kindness. Where there is poverty, oppressions, and bondage, help us to respond with justice. And when we are in need, O God, we pray that you would send others to care for and strengthen us in our journey.

We are all one in Christ. Enable us to celebrate our unity by caring for one another. And enable us to confess that Jesus is the Christ. Amen.

Exodus 1:8-2:10   Matthew 16:13-20

Sometimes, O God, we give up praying when we don't feel that you have heard us. And yet we are told to pray unceasingly. Often we don't know how to do that. So many distractions in our daily lives pull us away from our time with you. Sometimes we are afraid to be alone with you...afraid of solitude...even afraid of what we might hear. In those times of solitude and silence we are drawn away from the compulsions of this world and we begin to see things differently. We begin to see with the mind of Christ. We begin to open our hearts and minds to your loving care. And we begin to claim the promise of unceasing prayer...the promise that when we ask, it will be given to us. When we search for you, we will find you and your will find us. When we knock, you will open the door to surround us with welcoming arms.

And so we come to you this morning. We come asking, searching, and knocking. We come in prayer for all those things that rest heavily on our hearts. We lift prayers for our world, for peace among nations, and for justice for all your children. We lift prayers for our country and its leaders, that they might be guided in their decision-making and that they might govern with compassion and understanding. We lift prayers for those people we know and for those who remain unnamed to us. May the lonely find fellowship, the grief-stricken find comfort, the homeless find shelter, the ill find healing, the angry find inner peace, and the alienated be brought back into community. And finally, O God, we lift prayers for ourselves. May our faith be renewed, may we experience grace, and may we rest securely in your loving presence. Still our anxious hearts. Help us to be still and know that you are God. Purify us, liberate us, and transform us into the persons you would have us be in the name of the one who came to dwell among us, even Jesus Christ, our Lord. Amen.

Luke 11:5-13

O God, we come to you this day in a spirit of praise and thanksgiving for all the blessings you have bestowed upon us. We thank you for your promise to love us always and for your promise of the Holy Spirit. The Holy Spirit abide with us as Counselor, Comforter, and Helper. Sometimes we think, O God, that we have to do something to get the Spirit. Help us to experience the sense of peace that comes from knowing that we do not have to earn your love and grace by what we do or say. Rather the Spirit is a gift to all who are open to receiving your presence in their lives.

Help us to remember all that Jesus said and did, that we might be reminded of all that Christ charges us to do. We want to fulfill that charge. But sometimes our hearts are troubled, our minds unsettled, our spirits confused. Comfort us, quiet us, focus us, that we might rest in peace in your ever-loving arms. Grant us peace to entrust our lives to the guidance of your Holy Spirit, that we might not only see your light, but follow. Let your light shine on all who struggle in darkness: the addicted, the homeless, the unemployed, the exploited. Whatever stands in the way of their walking with dignity, help us to remove it. Let your light shine on all who are troubled or afraid: the sick, those who grieve, those in troubled relationships, those facing an uncertain future. Move us out of complacency through your indwelling spirit and enable us to minister to those in need of a hope to carry on. And lastly, O God, let your light shine on us. Help us in the discernment process to know your will for our lives and give us the courage to step out in faith and follow. When we hear your word to us, help us to obey. And grant that we might feel in our hearts a peace that surpasses all understanding as we put our whole trust in your grace and love. In the name of your Son, we lift our prayers. Amen.

John 14:23-29

112

God, our lives are surrounded by walls. Some walls are good and strong and keep things in where they should be. But other walls keep people out. We confess that too often we build walls made of fear, anger, misunderstanding and hatred. Too often we build walls to protect ourselves from being hurt, from being changed or from being vulnerable. In our blindness and prejudice, we forget the gates, doors, and windows in our walls.

Help us, Divine Spirit, to build walls that are freeing...walls that set boundaries of love and responsibility within which we may live and love and play. Help us, Loving God, not to be so quick to judge others. Help us to not create boundaries which separate us from your love for us, but rather enable us to trust in the protective walls that you provide. For your protection never fails and your divine walls of grace and love stand forever.

Heal our judging spirits, we pray, and make us forgiving people, shaped within your transforming love. Be with us as we build up and take down the many walls in our lives. Grant us the wisdom to know when to construct, when to confront, when to climb, when to dismantle, when to ignore, and when to go around the wall of our lives. And help us to remember that some of our walls may actually be bridges, answers to unspoken prayer. Amen.

Joshua 6:1-5   Ephesians 2:13-22

reator God, we are an anxious people. So often we spend our time dreading the difficulties of today and anticipating the problems of tomorrow. Changes in our world, and in our lives, often overwhelm us. We try to regain a sense of control. We seek to accumulate material things. We try to possess other people. We act in controlling ways. As long as things go along fairly smoothly, we can even fool ourselves into thinking we can handle everything alone.

Then we are faced with one of those unexpected changes and challenges and we are overcome by frustration and despair. And so here we are again, running back to you, Divine Spirit, seeking communion with you, seeking strength and courage, seeking again to follow your will. And we find you have never left. You are ever-present, knowing our needs, quieting our fears.

Once again we let go of our fear and anxiety and put our trust in you. Once again we are refreshed, renewed, restored and reconciled. Once again we are empowered to face the change and uncertainty in our lives. Once again you awaken us with your grace and we regain a sense of wonder. Like Abraham and Sarah, you enable us, once again, to step out in faith with the assurance that you walk with us.

Help us, O God, to find again a sense of hope and future, that in Christ all things are possible. Free us from our anxiety that we might be freed to become your disciples, trusting in you for all our needs rather than relying on the earthly treasures we cling to so tightly. Make us ready. Open our eyes, our ears and our hearts as we watch and wait for your light to shine in those unexpected times and places. Amen.

Hebrews 11:1-3, 8-12   Luke 12:32-40

Creator God, like a potter you framed the universe and formed us with your loving touch. You continue to mold and fashion our lives that we might be vessels of beauty and grace. You craft our talents and implant them within us. You restore us when we are broken. You remold us when we have gone astray. And so, Loving Creator, we yield to your touch, for you are the potter and we are the clay.

Into your hands we place our lives with all the tensions, difficulties and fragmentations and busyness as well as all the joys of health, family, friends and the opportunity for new beginnings.

Into your hands we place our church as we seek to care for the hurting and as we seek to grow in our faith. Help us to know that we need not depend on good deeds and possessions for our worth, for each of us is accepted and loved just as we are.

Into your hands we place our friends and families. Be with those who are hurting, the sorrowing, the struggling child, the frustrated parent, the fragile marriage. Teach us the sacrament of care in daily acts of love.

Into your hands we place our world, especially where there is brokenness and fighting. We pray for those yearning for justice, freedom and dignity of life. Show us the path of peace and the ways of sharing a brighter vision.

And so, this morning, we acknowledge that you are the potter and we are the clay. Mold us and make us after thy will, while we are waiting, yielded and still. Have thine own way, Lord. Amen.

Jeremiah 18:1-11

Divine Spirit, as we run the race of life, we often come across those hurdles, obstacles and difficult hills that weaken our spirit and test our faith. We grow weary, O God, as we come upon those disappointments and as we meet resistance, both within and without. Too often we lose sight of where we are going...of the finish line. And yet we are not alone. You are present with us in our triumphs, our trials and our defeats.

We thank you today for those who have run the course before us as well as for those who run beside us. Too often we find ourselves wrapped up in our own problems and we forget to look to those around us. And yet, because of those who have run before us and those who run with us, we realize that we do not need to solve the problems of this world all by ourselves. All these persons help us endure and persevere. For this we give you thanks.

You, O God, have provided us with a community of faith. Not only are we strengthened in our own faith journey, but you have provided a way for us to do our part to make peace a reality for all creation. Enable us, O God of Compassion, to run with and uphold those persons whose spirits have been crushed by the many adversities of life. Empower us, O God of Justice, to work against the forces of evil and oppression in whatever forms they might take. Encourage us, O God of Love, to strive for justice and peace as we care for each other and as we care for the gift of the created world which you have entrusted to our care. Help us to be ever alert and watchful as we look to Jesus as the perfector of our faith. Amen.

Hebrews 12:1-2

God, we are a murmuring people. Just as the Israelites murmured against Moses, so we murmur against one another, against our leaders, against the daily struggles we encounter in our personal lives. We are good at fault finding...at putting the blame on someone or something else. We easily get caught up in our own self-righteousness. And we murmur. And we thirst.

We thirst, O God, for that foundation, that rock, upon which our church was built. We thirst for your touch of grace, of hope, of forgiveness, of promise. We give you thanks that you leave us not alone in our times of thirst and temptation. For it is your Spirit that comforts us in our distress and goads us to action when our commitment falters.

Divine Spirit, make us mindful once again of the living water that enlivens our faith. Enable us, like Peter, to get our commitments and values straight, to make our confession of faith in Christ as our redeemer and savior. Especially in this time of tension and unrest in our world, may we be empowered by Christ's Spirit...a Spirit that thwarts oppression with an embracing love and concern for all people. We ask your special presence with our world leaders, with the innocent victims of violence and oppression, with all the families who are living with fear and uncertainty. May we be instruments of your peace. May we be grounded in Christ as the source of our lives. Only then will our thirst be quenched and our murmuring quieted. For on this rock "the powers of death shall not prevail." On this sure foundation, we confess our faith. Amen.

Exodus 17:1-7   Matthew 16:13-20

O God, there are those times in our lives when we feel empty, alone, even abandoned. There are those times when we feel overwhelmed by the constant barrage of demands made upon our time and energy. There are those times when we know in our hearts that we have failed to be the persons you have called us to be, and our shortcomings weigh heavy upon us.

These are the times, Loving Creator, when we need to be reminded of your promises to us. We need to be reminded that you created us and formed us and you call each one of us by name. You have claimed us as your children. We are your own. When we face despair, trials, suffering, uncertainty, fear or loneliness, you are with us and we can be comforted that these things will not overwhelm us. You hold us in your loving arms. We are precious in your eyes. For these promises you have made to us, we lift our praise and thanksgiving...and our prayers.

In you alone, we place our trust. Fill us with your loving presence. O Lord, hear us, we pray. O Lord, give us your love.

Grant us patience in all that we endure, that we may follow you more closely. O Lord, hear us, we pray. O Lord, give us your love.

Teach us to bear one another's burdens, and so fulfill your law of love. O Lord, hear us, we pray. O Lord, give us your love.

Send your Holy Spirit upon your Church. Guide and uphold all who you claim as your people. O Lord, hear us, we pray. O Lord, give us your love.

Renew our hearts in dedication to your will. Send your Spirit to all of your children. O Lord, hear us, we pray. O Lord, give us your love.

As your children, we are renewed and restored to go into the world to be witnesses to your love and presence in our lives. You have called us to be a light for the world and the salt of the earth. All glory to you, Almighty God, and to the Son, and to the Holy Spirit. As it was in the beginning, is now and ever shall be, world without end. Amen.

Isaiah 43:1-7   Matthew 5:13-16

Loving God, we come into your presence aware of an empty space within, aware that we need this time to be in quiet communion with you. And while we are comforted in our needs by the knowledge of your presence, you also challenge us. You shake us out of our comfortable ways of thinking and acting and force us to look at and reorder the priorities in our lives. We are not comfortable with Jesus' answer to the rich man's question of what he must do to inherit eternal life. It's the same question we carry in our hearts, if not on our lips. And so, we struggle with our values about our material wealth, about how we are using our gifts and talents, about how we spend our time.

Yet, you understand our struggle. Even though your word to us often feels sharper than a two-edged sword and is able to judge the thoughts and intentions of our hearts, you still come to us in love, just as Jesus loved the rich man. You must feel great sadness when we turn away from the gift of abundant life that you offer us because of our lack of trust, our lack of faith and our fear of letting go. But you love us still and continue to open to us new possibilities, where we learn that, with you, all things are possible.

And so today, O God, we ask that you rekindle in us the desire to be your faithful followers. Help us make strong the bonds of caring support within this church family so that we have the strength and commitment to minister to others. Enable us to move beyond the beauty of this sanctuary into our fractured world in order to heal where there is sickness, to feed where there is hunger, to reconcile where there is division and to proclaim your truth where there is ignorance. By your grace, through your Spirit and with your love, lead us into the future and make us what we are capable of becoming. In meeting the spiritual and physical needs of others, may we celebrate the power and goodness of this church in mission. Amen.

Hebrews 4:12-16   Mark 10:17-31

ternal God, we are once again overcome by the many blessings you have bestowed upon us. You have asked us to be faithful stewards of our earth, caring for our environment and all the created world. You call us to be faithful stewards of our financial resources, using our money wisely, rather than treating it as a measure of worth or accomplishment. You call us to be faithful stewards of our relationships with others, in our families, our places of work and with our friends. We especially lift up all those persons we know who are in need of healing, of forgiveness, of a loving word, of a chance to begin again. You call us to be a faithful people even when we think no one is looking or noticing. For you come to us, Spirit God, when we least expect you, in surprising ways, in those unlikely places.

Forgive us, O God, when we take advantage of the freedoms offered to us. Forgive us when we make poor choices that hurt ourselves and others. Forgive us when we grumble at our responsibilities and challenges because we think they are too demanding. We pray for courage to ask where the path of true discipleship may lead us. We pray for trust to live out the answer you provide with joy, as we embrace the risks, changes and new demands made upon us.

Teach us, Gentle Spirit, to be your voice, your feet and your hands upon this earth. Enable us to be faithful stewards of all the treasures you have placed in our care. For it is in faith that we find peace and in living for others that we find meaning for our own lives. Amen.

Matthew 24:45-51

God, we are but clay in your hands. You have placed a treasure deep inside each of us-a moment of insight, a touch of compassion, a sense of your unending love. We have been given the precious gift of caring for each other, of guarding each other's light and of proclaiming the wonder of your love and grace.

At times, we confess, this is not easy. We become blinded to our own treasure and worth. We become blinded to the strengths and gifts of others. We become afflicted with so many burdens-the burden of grief, the trials of illness, the confusion of youth, the weariness of age, the disappointment of rejection. The depressing headlines threaten to crush our spirits into inactivity and apathy.

Divine Spirit, may your light shine through our times of darkness, of despair, of death. May your Spirit work among us to heal us and move us toward new life and new beginnings. May we be empowered to see with the eyes of Christ.

We entrust to you once again, the earthen vessels of our lives. Center us, shape us, form us. Transform us into new creations. Save us from the death of everything grown old, cold and repetitious. May we experience new life through dying to old ways and patterns that destroy rather than build. Give us life in your Son. Use the earthen vessels of our lives to reflect your presence, light, and love in this world. Amen.

Jeremiah 18:1-6

2 Cor. 4:7-12

Divine Spirit, we come to you aware of our unfaithfulness. We have turned so easily to false prophets. We have made idols of our possessions, our power and our authority. Even as we turn away from you, you do not give up on us. You take us up in your arms like a parent cradles a child. You lead us with cords of compassion and bands of love. You ease our yoke and our burden. You bend down and feed us with nourishment for our weary souls.

We are humbled, O God, by your gift of grace on our behalf. Teach us to walk in faith, to love justice and to be steadfast in our commitments. We desire to serve you. Our failings weigh heavy on our hearts. We turn to you in this time, O Faithful One, in search of insight, clarity, and discernment in our renewed commitment to you. We will not be halfway in our intentions. We will not serve two masters.

And so we lift our prayers to you. Our world is in need of your healing balm. Your people war against one another. Your people are divided by color, creed, class, and culture. Bring unity where there is division, understanding where there is mistrust, and love where there is hate. We pray for all who are entrusted with the authority of government that they might withstand the pressures of office and rule with wisdom and justice. We pray for all who are burdened with sorrow and pain. Hear their cries for help and answer them. We pray for those who are experiencing loss of all kinds, whether it be as a result of natural disaster, death, illness or broken human relationships. We pray for our youth, for single persons and for all who struggle to find meaning and purpose in their lives. We pray for ourselves that we might be more faithful in our love for you. And we thank you, Holy Spirit, for guiding us safely through every trial and tribulation. We thank you for not giving up on us and for your great compassion for us. Amen.

Hosea 11:1-11   Luke 16:1-13

God, the Holy One in our midst, we rejoice in the prophet's message of hope. We rejoice and give thanks for your compassion and goodness in spite of our disobedience. Like a parent, you celebrate our small steps and new discoveries. Like a parent, you are ever-patient with our mistakes and our willfulness. You withhold your anger when we are unfaithful, and you love us with a love that knows no limits.

Today, in your presence, we are once again aware of our many shortcomings. We are once again called to examine our lives, to change our hearts and to move forward in new directions that enhance life rather than destroy life. We are once again called to respond to your goodness and mercy by reaching out to others in need.

We are reminded, O God, of your presence and reassurance even as we make our requests to you in prayer. So today we lift prayers, not only for ourselves, but for all of your children everywhere. We lift up all those persons facing shattered homes and shattered dreams. We lift those persons whose lives are troubled in ways known only to you...by broken relationships, poverty, disease, by uncertain futures and by difficult decisions. We lift up those persons in high positions who are involved in political considerations that affect our global world. We even lift up, O God, those persons who do not believe as we do, and even those who are against us. Help us to understand that your love, compassion and grace extend beyond our parochial attitudes to encompass all of creation. Fill us anew with your Holy Spirit that we might be your faithful children. Amen.

reator God, we come to you this day so aware that we are surrounded by your gifts...gifts that we often take for granted. We are richly blessed in so many ways, and yet, in the midst of the struggles and challenges of our daily lives, we often overlook the moments of blessing and the small miracles happening before our eyes. We are blinded to your presence as we focus on our losses, rather than on your gifts of grace.

And so we offer to you, Divine Healer, those hurts and losses that hold us back from trusting fully in your love for us. We ask your healing presence be with those of us who feel the loss of a relationship, the loss of a loved one, the loss of a job, the loss of health, the loss of a dream, the loss of a place to call home. We offer to you our struggling prayer life, the doubts that come upon us and sometimes overwhelm us. We come to you out of our need to be in community and relationship with you and with others. For we know, O God, that when we turn to you in our poverty of spirit and in our weakness, you are there to offer an abundance of grace. When we turn to you in our emptiness, our loneliness and our times of personal need, you are there to offer healing, wholeness and the chance to begin again.

Enable us, we pray, to be vulnerable enough to face the truth, to be courageous enough to take risks and to have faith enough to put our trust, and our very lives, into your loving care. In doing so, may we move beyond our own needs, to be vessels of your love and carriers of your hope to others. Your Spirit frees us to love others and to care for our created world. Like the widow, we offer to you our small, limited and fumbling efforts to reach out in compassion to the world in response to your great love for us. May we trust that when we have given all, we are not left empty. Rather, when we put our trust in your grace, we find that you take the little we have and transform it into abundance. Amen.

1 Kings 17:8-16   Mark 12:38-44

oly One, we come into your presence to listen for and discern your word to us. For we seek to respond to the Spirit moving among us and within us. Keep us attentive to your voice and quick to perceive your call in the events and people we encounter in our daily lives.

We hear your commandment, "You shall love your neighbor as yourself," and we are challenged to make our faith a faith of action and commitment. We are challenged, first of all, to really love ourselves the way you love us. For many of us this is difficult. We have been told we are unworthy, or we feel guilty for our sins of commission or omission, but if we are to live as recipients of your abundant love and grace, we must learn first to accept ourselves.

And then, Loving God, you challenge us to love our neighbors. For many of us this is difficult as well, especially when our neighbor is different from us in some way. Forgive us our indifference to the sounds of a hurting world. Forgive us our blindness to the sight of your wounded people. Forgive us our silence when a word of justice needs to be spoken. Unstop our ears, open our eyes and loose our tongues that we may have the courage to speak the truth and to act decisively when we are confronted with cries for justice and scars of oppression.

May we, like the Syrophoenician woman, live a life of faith and trust, but also be persistent and expectant that Christ came to make all persons whole regardless of race, gender, age or social status. If we truly believed and acted on the truth that each person has dignity and worth, there would be no need for the secrecy Jesus requested after his healings. Healing and wholeness would be a living reality rather than a proclaimed and hoped-for desire. May we be co-creators with you, O God, in making your Kingdom come on earth, as it is in heaven. Amen.

James 2:1-10, 14-17   Mark 7:24-37

Loving God, you have created such a wonderful world for us. You have created us and called us your own. How we long to know you better. We search for you. We search for meaning and purpose in our lives.

In doing so, we are not so different from the chief priests and the elders who were anxious about authority. We are not so different from the Pharisees whose worry about Caesar transcended their worship of you. We are not so different from the Sadducees, whose concern about the future life dwarfed their interest in the here and now. And so we question and wonder. What is right? What is correct? What is just?

O God, grant to us the understanding of the scribe who questioned Jesus, not because of suspicion, but in faith. Let us ask, with him, "Which commandment is the first of all?" And when you answer that we are to love God and our neighbor and ourselves, enable us to embrace your answer and courageously live the kind of life to which we have been called. May your commandment of love be written on our hearts and may we go forth to write its message on the heart of the world.

Guide us, Loving Spirit. Calm our fears. Be with those of us who are hurting in some way...a way known only to you. Be with those who are ill in body, mind, or spirit. Comfort those who have lost a loved one. Strengthen those who seek discernment in making a difficult decision. Enable us to love our neighbors by seeking justice and compassion in this fragmented world.

We, like the scribe, seek the Kingdom of God. By your grace, enable us to catch a glimpse of that Kingdom in our lives this day. All this we ask in the name of the Risen Christ. Amen.

Mark 12:28-34

ou come to us in this day and in this hour, O God, bringing justice and righteousness, bringing hope and comfort. You know our weaknesses. Sometimes we are wise, sometimes foolish. Sometimes we are watchful, at other times, careless. Sometimes we are alert. At other times we are unprepared and unaware. We have wasted your precious gifts of minutes and hours. We have been distracted by the insignificant. We have fretted and worried away the hours, and we have put off the important, always believing there would be more time.

And so we pray, O God of Wisdom, that you would forgive our foolishness and touch our inmost being once again. Challenge our comfortable routines and attitudes. Equip us with oil for our lamps, hope in the midst of grief, and renewed purpose when we are weighted down with despair.

Help us to be prepared for Christ's coming among us. Help us to be patient while we wait and serve. Help us to see your light in the midst of our darkness. Help us to lift the heavy burdens of our neighbors. And help us to do what we can to replace hatred with love, self-centeredness with sharing, and the prospects of war, with peace.

In all the times of our lives, we stand together as your people, to give comfort to one another and to lift up our hope in Christ. Be with us in our times of watchfulness. Keep us alert and prepared so we do not miss the many surprises you have in store for each of us. Keep us ever ready to see your light and to trust in your grace. Amen.

Matthew 25:1-13

Mother's Day

Today, O God, as we celebrate Mother's Day, and lift up the Christian home, we are filled with a variety of feelings, emotions, and memories. We give you thanks for the tender times when our mothers and fathers have mirrored your love for us. We remember them driving us to ball games and scouts, encouraging us with our homework, putting bandages on skinned knees, hugging our hurt pride, waiting up for us to come home at night. We remember these ordinary, everyday expressions of love and our hearts are warmed.

But it is also a time for painful memories, of families torn apart, of family members losing their way, of separation and divorce, of couples unable to have children, of loneliness in the midst of many. And we remember with sadness those parents no longer with us where, perhaps, there was so much more we would have wanted to say. We ask, Loving God, that you would ease our hurtful family memories and restore to us a sense of your love.

For we are your children, your chosen ones. No matter what our family situation, we give thanks for our special place in your family. Continue to hold us in your tender embrace. For the times we have failed to cherish and use the gifts you have given to each of us, we ask your forgiveness. For the times we have failed to encourage the gifts and growth of others close to us, we ask your forgiveness. Guide us, Loving Parent, that we might live as your children, full of the awe and wonder of all that life offers.

And so on this morning we lift our prayers first of all for all mothers and fathers, grandmothers and grandfathers, sisters and brothers. We especially celebrate with new parents who are just beginning a journey of love. We lift prayers for those we know who are hurting, who suffer with illness, who struggle with hard decisions, who grieve losses and past memories, who are confused about what to do next with their lives. We lift prayers for families who face loss. We lift prayers for the leaders of our country that they might support those things that strengthen and uphold families. But mostly, we ask your help, O God, in committing ourselves anew to living out the sort of unconditional love within our families that makes real the meaning of your steadfast and abiding love for us. Amen.

Mother's Day

Spirit of the Living God, fall afresh on us. Come upon us this day, we pray, as you came upon the disciples of old. Help us to feel your spirit blow through us...a spirit that binds us in covenant and communion with you and with all your sons and daughters of every time and place.

Touch us with the fiery flames of enthusiasm that we might be empowered by your spirit to work for justice and truth, for freedom and love. Touch us and strengthen us with your compassion that we might be made channels of love, healing, comfort, and hope to others.

We thank you, Divine Spirit, for the many gifts you bring to us. We are especially thankful this day for all mothers...for young mothers who are just beginning the journey with hardship along the way; for mothers who have died but whose spirit remains such a vital presence in our lives. Awaken in us all, men and women alike, a mothering, nurturing spirit toward one another and toward all creation.

We thank you also, O God, for the gift of families...for the love shared and for the gift of children. Help all of us to renew our commitment to nurture the growth and development of those who share our homes with us.

May we not get too busy or too harried or too preoccupied with the details of everyday life that we fail to feel the gentle breeze of your Spirit. Continue to surprise us and renew us this day and every day that we might be continually opened to your presence in our midst. We pray these things in the name and spirit of the living God made known to us in Jesus Christ. Amen.

Mother's Day

racious God, you have called us to be faithful disciples. You have given us tasks to perform. You have equipped us with gifts and abilities beyond what we deserve. You have called us to work in the vineyards of our offices, our schools, our church, our community, and our families. Yet we often grumble and complain. We often find ourselves feeling jealous and competitive. We find ourselves becoming more concerned with personal reward than with accomplishing the tasks you have set before us. We find ourselves resentful of what others receive. And we overlook, and even forget, your grace and generosity in our lives.

We give you thanks, Compassionate God, that you see beyond our petty grumbling and continue to shower us with blessings and to bestow upon us the gift of your unconditional love. You have chosen us, adopted us as your children, and called us into this community as the family of Christ. We are so grateful this day, Parent God, that you have placed us in the vineyard of the family where your love for us has a human face. We especially lift up mothers this morning. We celebrate and give thanks for new mothers who have experienced pain and hardship along that journey.

O God, whom we know as our Divine Parent, we are grateful for all those persons, mothers and fathers, sisters and brothers, grandparents, and others with whom we share the special relationships of the family. Strengthen and support our families, we pray, in the daily tasks of love. Amen.

Labor Day

Creator God, As we gather together this Labor Day weekend, we give thanks for the opportunities you give us to minister in our various jobs. Help us to always be aware of how our lives are linked with others that we might continually be aware of the needs and aspirations of our fellow workers.

Open our hearts, O God, as we remember those who suffer want and anxiety from the lack of work. Guide the people of this land to so use our public and private wealth that all may find suitable and fulfilling employment, and grant that all may receive just payment for their labor.

Empower us, Sustainer God, to be a reflection of your steadfast love to all with whom we come in contact. Help us to be open to the many opportunities we have to be in ministry to others-with our families and friends, in our place of work, and in our times of relaxation and recreation.

We remember also this day those persons who need your presence in a special way. We remember the leadership of our country and our world, the leadership of Christ's universal Church, those who are oppressed, imprisoned, hungry, or lonely. We remember those in need of your spiritual as well as physical healing.

As we celebrate the end of summer, we look forward with a sense of expectancy as many of us return to school or to new jobs. We are thankful for the new beginnings and new chances that you constantly provide for us. O God, our strength and redeemer, accept the prayers of your people, and strengthen us to do your will. Amen.

Labor Day

O God, we come before you this Labor Day Sunday with a mixture of feelings. Many of us give thanks for meaningful work, for the opportunity to use the gifts you have given us to bring your Kingdom a little closer. But others of us come today filled with anxiety. Some of us worry about job security. Others of us are unemployed in this time of economic uncertainty.

Enable us to move beyond concerns for ourselves and those things that possess us, to live in the Spirit, trusting that you will provide for all of our needs. Free us to become aware of relationships, patterns, and surprises that make our lives meaningful. Help us to be more fully yours, that we may be more completely open and receptive to all your gifts. Make us aware of all that we have to give to the world around us even as we lift our prayers to you this day.

We lift prayers, first of all, for a special person or circumstance that is in our heart this day. In your mercy, Lord, hear our prayers.

We lift prayers of care and compassion for all who suffer loss. Move us beyond our good intentions to act on behalf to others. In your mercy, Lord, hear our prayers.

We lift prayers for all those who have lost hope, for those broken in spirit, for the poor, the hungry, the dying, the disenfranchised and the imprisoned. Give them a vision of a new beginning in your grace. In your mercy, Lord, hear our prayers.

We pray for those individuals and families touched by illness. May their troubled spirits find peace in your presence. In your mercy, Lord, hear our prayers.

We pray for ourselves that we might joyfully accept the demands that discipleship places upon us. Help us to sow seeds for the good of all. In your mercy, Lord, hear our prayers.

God of freedom and grace, center us in your grace so that we might let go of all that enslaves us. Enable us to be open to the inbreaking of your surprising love. Fill us with hope and confidence and give us the courage to reap a harvest of blessing. Amen.

Galatians 6:7-10

World Communion Sunday

Gracious God, we come together as Christians from all over the world to share in the bounty of your table. We gather to share the cup of life and the bread that provides strength for our journey. We gather speaking many languages and worshiping you in ways unique to our culture and heritage. But in our diversity, there is unity. No where else, Loving God, are we made more aware of how interconnected we really are, than at your table. The bread and cup, symbols of Christ's broken body, speak to us of the broken bodies in the world today which cry out for the healing power of your spirit. And so we humbly offer to you our lives and our spirits, just as we are, knowing that you can use our brokenness to bring about healing and wholeness in your name.

On this World Wide Communion Sunday, we lift our prayers to you, knowing that you already hear the yearnings of our hearts.

We lift prayers for our global neighbors, especially those persons living in fear or poverty, and for those who have lost hope. Give us the courage to recognize and name the pain of our global neighbors and to reach out where we can. In your mercy, Lord, hear our prayers.

We lift prayers for our earth that we all share, and that you have entrusted to us to nurture and care for. Enable us to use our power wisely as our earth is reaching the point of being unable to feed its people and because land is being destroyed by greed, careless development, and erosion. In your mercy, Lord, hear our prayers.

We lift prayers for those close to us, some of whom we name in our hearts...the sick, the addicted, the abused, the imprisoned, the depressed, and those grieving some loss in their life. May they be comforted and fed by the bread and cup of new life. In your mercy, Lord, hear our prayers.

We lift prayers for ourselves and for our society that puts so much worth on material wealth and possessions. Free us so that we can learn to receive and give with equal joy. In your mercy, Lord, hear our prayers.

Pour out your Spirit upon all the nations of the earth and upon all whom you have named and claimed as your own in Christ's name. For all the blessings in our lives and for your promise to always be with us, we lift our prayers of praise and thanksgiving. Amen.

Youth Sunday

We give thanks today, O God, for the journey of life with each of its stage of growth and opportunity. We give thanks for childhood, with its sense of wonder and discovery. We give thanks for adolescence, with its miracle of growth and new relationships. We give thanks for mid-life, with its adaptations and changes. And we give thanks for later years, with their joy and fulfillment and even their new beginnings. It is a pilgrimage of learning and experience, but no matter where we find ourselves on the journey, we give thanks for your presence with us. We never journey alone.

Guide us, Loving Creator, in our daily walk. Teach us to rise above our mistakes and move on. Enable us to forgive our enemies, to cherish friends and to love adventure. Inspire us to live to the fullest, both individually and in community. Let the talents, wisdom, and love you have given us find rich expression in our work and play and in our daily relationships.

On this Sunday, we especially celebrate and lift up our youth. This is a difficult time for them to grow up in, with many pressures and much confusion. They receive conflicting messages from parents and teachers, from peers, and from the media. The temptations are numerous. Help them, Divine Spirit, to make choices and to seek values that would lead them into a closer walk with your purposes. Grant them a sense of your presence to go with them wherever their journeys lead, to watch over them, and to lead them in paths of righteousness and fulfillment.

Give each of us the grace, O God, to reach out to each other, young and old alike, that we might discover anew the compassion, the patience, and the love which brings us ever closer to your kingdom here on earth. Amen.

Stewardship Sunday

Loving Creator, as we focus this morning on stewardship and the future of this church, we are reminded of the many ways that you have blessed our lives. Daily we are reminded how bountiful your gifts really are, and so we pause, O God, to reflect on our response to your many blessings.

You have blessed us with the beauty of the earth and, in gratitude, we respond by blessing the earth through the practice of good stewardship of all the created world. You have blessed us with an unconditional love, and, in gratitude, we respond by blessing others through the sharing of our love and concern. We have been blessed with our physical bodies we so often take for granted, and, in gratitude, we respond by caring for our bodies and by lifting up those who are sick or hurting. We have been blessed with human love as expressed in our families and with friends, and, in gratitude, we respond by reaching out to those who feel alienated and alone. We have been blessed with our church, and, in gratitude, we respond by helping to keep our church vital and growing, that our church might be a source of blessing to a broken world.

We pray that our church might overflow with Christ's love in our community. You are a blessing God and have promised to be with us in all the times of our lives. In gratitude, we respond to your call to bless others as we recommit ourselves to the furtherance of your kingdom in all that we do and say. Amen.

Church Anniversary

This is a day of celebration! It is a time, O God, for remembering the past and giving thanks for the ministry of this church and for those faithful disciples whose spirit continues to move among us even today. We have been blessed by the witness of so many brothers and sisters in Christ, who willingly accepted the cost of discipleship and who risked to put their faith into action through this church.

Even as we celebrate the past, we are aware of your spirit calling us into the future. In the midst of celebration, we are called to take an accounting of our mission, or how we use our resources, of our response to the needs of others, of our commission to share the message of new life and hope. In the midst of celebration, Divine Spirit, we are called to recommit ourselves as a church family to the building of your kingdom on earth and especially in our city.

And so today, O God, we ask that you rekindle in us the desire to be your faithful followers. Help us make strong the bonds of caring support within this church family so that we have the strength and commitment to minister to others in the name of Christ. Enable us to move beyond the beauty of this sanctuary into our fractured world in order to heal where there is sickness, to feed where there is hunger, to reconcile where there is division, and to proclaim your truth where there is ignorance. By your grace, through your spirit, and with your love, lead us into the future and make us what we are capable of becoming. In meeting the spiritual and physical needs of others, may we celebrate the power and goodness of this church in mission. Amen.

All Saints' Day

God of love, we gather here this morning to praise you and declare your mercy. In times of despair we have been scattered by our sorrows, our mourning, our crying, and our pain. You have gathered us back together that we might feast with you in joy. When we were buried in despair, lifeless and without hope, you raised us up, proclaiming a love that is stronger than death. You have wiped the tears from our eyes. You make all things new and give us a vision of hope and promise for the future.

On this All Saints' Sunday we give you thanks for the witness of persons of faith, past and present. In every time and place, you have raised up men and women whose devotion and integrity inspired others to follow you. Thank you for the witness of Peter, upon whom you founded your church; for Mary, the first to proclaim the Good News of your resurrection; for those women in the early church who opened their homes as centers of mission and ministry. We thank you for the millions of disciples whose names are known only to you, who led their children, their neighbors and their friends to follow you in faith. Thank you for the courageous reformers of the church, for Luther, Calvin, Wesley, and Pope John the 23rd. Thank you for the sacrificial love of those who have served the sick, the wounded, the hungry, and the dying—those faithful servants like Mother Teresa whose work continues to this day. And we especially give thanks for those persons who have meant so much in our own lives and for the witness of their faith, their love, and their presence.

May we have the desire, the courage, and the strength, Loving God, to continue the great heritage of faith through our children and our children's children. Work though us and through them so that many may come to know the power of your love. Make us one with your saints in heaven and on earth. Grant that in our earthly pilgrimage we may always be supported by this fellowship of love and prayer. Amen.

All Saints' Day

God of the ages, we lift our hearts on this day of remembrance to praise you and to give thanks for all the saints who have stood in the faith before us. We thank you for the steadfast hope of the patriarchs and matriarchs of our faith. We thank you for the ministry of our Lord. We thank you for the Apostles who kept the faith through every trial and tradition. And we thank you for the long line of disciples through the centuries. We especially remember to give thanks for those most dear to us-fathers and mothers, brothers and sisters, children, cherished friends-who have been gathered up to life everlasting even as we continue our pilgrimages here on earth. We find comfort in your promise that "all will be made alive in Christ."

And so, Loving God, we open ourselves this day to your ceaseless outpouring of love. We awake each day to your presence. When we are anxious or troubled, you comfort us. When we are faced with difficult choices that confuse us, you are there to guide us. You have surrounded us with your love before we even turned to you. You are here now as we lift prayers to you.

We place before you our fragmented, busy lives. Teach us that we need not depend on our doing and having for our sense of worth. In your mercy, Lord, hear our prayers.

We place before you our friends—the hurt, the addicted, the sorrowing, the struggling child, the frustrated parent, the fragile marriage. Teach us the sacrament of care as we reach out to others in acts of love. In your mercy, Lord, hear our prayers.

We place before you our church. Teach us the way of trust and compassion and empower us to share the story of our faith where we live and work. In your mercy, Lord, hear our prayers.

We place before you our broken world, a world yearning for justice and freedom. Teach us the paths of peace and give us a brighter vision and hope for the future. In your mercy, Lord, hear our prayers.

Ever present God, you hear our prayers and astound us with your grace. Make us one with your saints in heaven and on earth. Grant that in our earthly pilgrimage we may always be supported by this fellowship of love and prayer. Amen.

1 Corinthians 15:12-22

All Saints' Day

God, on this All Saints' Sunday, we give you thanks that all of us, and all those who have gone before, can share in your riches of the "glorious inheritance in the saints." You have given us a hope and a vision through our faith in Jesus Christ that all "the saints of the Most High shall receive the Kingdom, and possess the Kingdom for ever, and ever." In grateful response, we lift prayers of praise and thanksgiving that we are linked to all the saints across the generations.

And yet, at the same time, we are aware of those forces that would cause us to be unfaithful. We look around and see people suffering. We see broken relationships. We see injustice and oppressions. We see illness and death. We see homelessness, people with AIDS, and persons struggling with addictions. We see this earth you have given us being used in an irresponsible way. We look around and see all these things and we wonder. We need, O God, your message of hope in the midst of our hurting lives and our hurting world. We need to be encouraged in the faith to endure the difficult times as those who have gone before us.

Even in the midst of our concerns, we are witnesses to your power and love. We see evidence of the new age already breaking in around us. And we realize that we share in the responsibility for making that new age a reality. We are called to be lovers of creation and healers of wounds. We are called to forgive wrongs and to offer blessing to others. We are called to share our faith in Jesus Christ and to live out our beliefs. Fill us, Divine Spirit, with the hope and confidence to face all the adversities of life. Give us courage to share our faith with others. Guide us in the right direction.

In all things, O God, you are the source of meaning in our lives. As the God of our ancestors, you fill us with joy and hope for the future. For you are our God and we are your people. Amen.

Thanksgiving Sunday

Loving God, Abundant Provider, you bless us with the gifts from the earth and you spread out goodness enough for all to share. On this day we join in public thanksgiving for the many blessings we enjoy even as we are mindful of the times when we stray, thinking we can go it alone and handle things ourselves. But in our emptiness, you call us home, celebrate and rejoice at our return and surround us with a grace that knows no limits.

You, O God, are the source of all good gifts. It is to you that we lift our prayers of grateful thanksgiving and our prayers of concern. We give thanks for this country and for all those who have gone before and labored to bring us the freedoms we enjoy. May our leaders today have the same vision to work for human dignity in all decisions that are made. In your mercy, Lord, hear our prayers.

We give thanks for family and friends and especially we thank you for those persons who have stood by us in our difficult times. We lift prayers for those who come to this holiday season grieving the loss of a loved one, even as we give thanks for the memories that sustain us in our loss. In your mercy, Lord, hear our prayers.

We give thanks for the laughter of children, for the joy we feel as we delight in your created world. We celebrate the wonder and mystery of the earth to plant, the sky to watch, the flowers to smell, and the trees that provide shelter and beauty. Forgive us for not working harder to protect these precious gifts. In your mercy, Lord, hear our prayers.

We give thanks for the opportunity for education and employment even as we lift up those persons who face economic uncertainty in an uncertain world. Ease their anxiety with the peace of your presence. In your mercy, Lord, hear our prayers.

We give thanks for the gift of our physical bodies, for the exhilaration of exercise and the benefits of health. But we also lift up those persons who struggle with pain and illness. Ease their burdens and bring healing of mind, body, spirit, and relationships. In your mercy, Lord, hear our prayers.

Deuteronomy 26:1-11

Scripture Reference Index